Dedicated to
John Steadman

Gentleman, friend, colleague, who was
always there for every block, tackle, pass and
kick, may this book honor his memory.

Book Staff

Editor
RAY FRAGER

Photography Editor
JIM PRESTON

Design Editor
VICTOR PANICHKUL

Photo Production
DENISE SANDERS

Project Manager
DEBORAH GOLUMBEK

THE BALTIMORE SUN

Published by:
The Baltimore Sun
A Tribune Company
501 N. Calvert St.
Baltimore, MD 21278

Hardcover ISBN 1-893116-21-2
Paperback ISBN 1-893116-20-4

Library of Congress Card Catalogue Number under application

GENE SWEENEY JR.

Contents

COVER PHOTO OF RAY LEWIS: GENE SWEENEY JR.

KENNETH K. LAM

Introduction

A purple kind of love

BY MIKE PRESTON

The love affair between an old, historic city in the NFL and its new professional football team was rekindled in the 2000 season.

An affection once reserved for the Baltimore Colts and its legends like John Unitas, Lenny Moore and John Mackey has extended to the Ravens and their modern-day stars Ray Lewis, Shannon Sharpe and Rod Woodson.

By the end of the season, the circle was complete. The Ravens' 34-7 win against the New York Giants in Super Bowl XXXV concluded a magical playoff run and put Baltimore on top of the football world again for the first time since the old Colts defeated the Dallas Cowboys, 16-13, in Super Bowl V in 1971.

As a sellout crowd of 71,921 at Raymond James Stadium in Tampa, Fla., and the rest of the world watched, the league's best defense shut down the Giants and the Ravens got big plays from cornerback Duane Starks, return specialist Jermaine Lewis and receiver Brandon Stokley to turn the game into a rout.

Ravens middle linebacker Ray Lewis was the game's Most Valuable Player, but the night also belonged to the fans of Baltimore, who'd suffered without an NFL team for 12 years after owner Robert Irsay slithered his team out of town to Indianapolis on a cold, March night in 1984.

The Colts created memories in Baltimore from 1947 through 1983, but the Ravens have formed their own special bond in a community that has gone Ravens crazy.

Purple-mania has arrived.

Local sporting goods stores sell out of team merchandise. Area schools hold Ravens days. Purple lights shine throughout a city whose mayor attended team practices during the playoffs. Young children paint their faces purple and black, and statues inside City Hall are clad in purple jerseys.

The street on which the team's practice facility is located was temporarily renamed Ravens Boulevard, and there aren't many conversations in bars where the talk doesn't turn to the Ravens.

"The response in this city to what we've done so far has been humongous," said Ravens owner Art Modell, who moved his franchise from Cleveland to Baltimore for the start of the 1996 season. "I've had many, many playoff games, four championships in Cleveland prior to this one, but nothing has turned a town on like we have witnessed in Baltimore. This city has been denied football for 12 years, and all their pent-up emotions were channeled toward the Eagles, Redskins, Jets, Giants and even Miami where they tried to find a kindred spirit.

"When we came in here in the dark days in Memorial Stadium, we didn't do too much either, but at least they had something to hang on to," said Modell. "The attachment grew, the romance grew to where it is now a full-grown love affair. Every player, every coach, cannot get over the response given to them. It has been overwhelming.

"It's euphoria personified," Modell said. "I've never seen a town so galvanized. White. Black. Rich. Poor. Cross-town. Uptown. Downtown. Everything has come together with a common rooting interest. It's magnificent. It's what football is all about. No other institution in this city or any city can do what this team is doing to this town right now."

The Ravens really had an amazing run to glory. There is hardly anyone, even the Ravens themselves, who believed they would play in, much less win, Super Bowl XXXV. The most reasonable scenario was an outside chance at the playoffs, especially with the defending AFC Central champion Jacksonville Jaguars and defending AFC champion Tennessee Titans in the same division.

But this is a story about a team whose best player, Ray Lewis, was involved in a double-murder trial in May and that had to play five of its first seven games on the road.

The Ravens shuffled quarterbacks, running backs and wide receivers during the regular season, a sure formula for disaster, and also endured five games without scoring a touchdown, losing three.

For an encore, they had to play successive road games against Tennessee in the AFC semifinals followed by the Oakland Raiders in the conference championship game.

It was always an uphill battle, but ended in Super Bowl victory.

"Never at any point did I feel we were out of it," said Ravens president David Modell. "Faith is faith. You have to have it. It's not like a library book where you can turn it in at any time at your own convenience."

Coach Brian Billick said: "There are a lot of things in the game that tear at the heart and fabric of the team concept — salary cap, free agency and the media to name a few. What allows you to handle and sometimes overcome all of this is chemistry and character. We have both of those in abundance. We have enough to stare into the abyss and grow strong.

"We did it when we went through our three-game losing streak and our touchdown drought," he said. "We've won with shutouts, and we've won with great comebacks at the ends of games, especially against Jacksonville at home and Tennessee in November."

Thank goodness for the defense and Pro Bowl place-kicker Matt Stover.

Defense was the team's most consistent weapon throughout the 2000 season. There will be debates for years about how this unit compares to other great defenses, such as the 1985 Chicago Bears and the Pittsburgh Steelers of the 1970s. But these facts can't be denied:

The Ravens set 16-game records in points allowed, 165, and rushing yards allowed, 970. They recorded four shutouts, one shy of the post-merger NFL record held by the 1976 Steelers. The Ravens finished first in the league in six defensive categories, and have not allowed a 100-yard rusher in the past 33 games.

And they have possibly the NFL's best player in Ray Lewis, who was named the Defensive Player of the Year.

But though Lewis is the most distinquished, the Ravens have other players with a blue-collar work ethic, like defensive tackle Tony Siragusa and defensive ends Michael McCrary and Rob Burnett. They also have potential superstars in outside linebacker Peter Boulware and cornerback Chris McAlister. The Ravens had three defensive players named to the AFC Pro Bowl squad in Lewis, free safety Rod Woodson and defensive tackle Sam Adams, a top free-agent acquisition in the off-season along with tight end Shannon Sharpe.

"They can say all they want about offense, but defense wins Super Bowls," said reserve defensive end Keith Washington. "When you can punch someone in the mouth like we do every week, it's a good thing. There is nothing wrong with that."

The Ravens tried a wide-open approach on offense earlier in the season, and it didn't work. The team jumped out to a 4-1 record, but the early signs of offensive trouble came in Game No. 5, when the Ravens had to rely on four field goals to beat the Cleveland Browns, 12-0.

The Ravens went four more games without a touchdown, losing the last three to the Washington Redskins, Tennessee and Pittsburgh. After losing 14-6 to the Titans, Billick benched starting quarterback Tony Banks for Trent Dilfer, who got similar results in the 9-6 loss to Pittsburgh.

The Ravens had wanted Banks to take control of the offense in 2000 after rallying the team to six wins in its last nine games during the 8-8 season of 1999. But Banks completed only 150 of 274 passes for 1,578 yards and eight touchdowns with eight interceptions in a disappointing 2000 season.

Banks, though, was only part of the problem. The Ravens had a wide-open approach but a new tight end in Sharpe, a rookie wide receiver in Travis Taylor and running back Jamal Lewis, the No. 5 overall draft pick last April, who didn't start the first three games of the season.

The national media ridiculed the Ravens during what Modell called "The Dust Bowl." But Billick was able to quell any dissension between his offensive and defensive players.

The p-word, as in playoffs, was silent.

"Obviously, that was the low point in the season," said McCrary. "But I think Brian did a good job of keeping us together, giving us confidence. We went from 5-1 to 5-4, and he said the same people laughing at us now we would be laughing at when we're 12-4."

Even some of the fans started to doubt.

"I guess to some degree we all started wondering what was going to happen, that we weren't going to get to Billick's promised land," said Fred Henson, 33, of Sykesville. "I didn't stop watching or rooting for them, but I did lose some hope."

The Ravens came out of the touchdown funk on Nov. 5 with a 27-7 win against the Cincinnati Bengals, and then pulled a major upset a week later by defeating Tennessee, 24-23, to become the first team to defeat the Titans at Adelphia Coliseum.

The Ravens followed with two more convincing wins, 27-0 against the Dallas Cowboys and 44-7 over Cleveland, but the passing offense went into a mini-slump during the last three games of the regular season. It was then that Billick, who has often been criticized for being too cute on offense with his "explosive" and "vertical plays," seemed to realize that the team's formula for success would be to combine dominating defense with a ball-control offense.

A star was born in Jamal Lewis, who in the final eight regular-season games (all wins), had 1,254 yards from scrimmage, representing almost half of the Ravens' 2,837 total net yards.

The defense, which had yielded 309 total yards to the Arizona Cardinals and 524 to the New York Jets in the final two games of the regular season, turned up the intensity in the playoffs.

The Ravens, in the first NFL playoff game in Baltimore since 1977, held Denver to 177 total yards in the wild-card game, a 21-3 Ravens win. The odds seemed to be stacked against the Ravens playing the Titans on the road in the conference semifinals, but the Ravens blocked two field goals and special teams player Anthony Mitchell returned one of those 90 yards for a touchdown. Ray Lewis also returned an intercepted pass 50 yards in the fourth quarter in the stunning, 24-10 victory.

Oakland was a six-point favorite in the AFC championship game, and the Raiders had the most balanced offense and rowdiest fans in the league. But the Ravens held the league's No. 1 rushing attack to 24 yards and got a 96-yard touchdown catch from Sharpe on a 10-yard pass in a 16-3 victory.

The Ravens don't win pretty. Sharpe become virtually the team's only offensive weapon in the playoffs. He caught a twice-batted pass and ran 58 yards for a touchdown against Denver. In the playoff game against Tennessee, Sharpe set up the Ravens' only touchdown, a 1-yard run by Lewis, on a 56-yard reception down the left sideline.

It's those kinds of plays and turnovers that worked in the Ravens' favor all year. It's those kinds of plays that made Baltimore fans believe the Ravens were a team of destiny. They were, winning Super Bowl XXXV easily on a 38-yard touchdown reception by Stokley in the first quarter, a 49-yard interception return for a touchdown by Starks in the third quarter and an electrifying, momentum-killing, 84-yard kickoff return from Jermaine Lewis 36 seconds after Starks' heroics.

The win could make Baltimore a football town again, just like it was when the Colts were here.

"I was here in the late '60s when the Colts went to the Super Bowl," said Harvey Kettering, 45, a food technologist from Baltimore. "Those were the days when the Colts ruled Baltimore even though the Orioles were a good team and going to the playoffs. I think the Ravens will rule the city again."

"At the beginning, I didn't believe we were going to be that good," said Evelyn Boricm, 37, of Cockeysville. "This just makes me realize that miracles can happen."

Sign of popularity

LLOYD FOX

Fans at the Ravens' Westminster training camp show no decreased enthusiasm for Ray Lewis.

Fitting in

LLOYD FOX

Free-agent acquisition Shannon Sharpe brought a Super Bowl winner's perspective to the Ravens.

September 3, 2000 • Three Rivers Stadium, Pittsburgh

Ravens drop their own curtain on Steelers

By Ken Murray

PITTSBURGH — The Ravens won here last year with explosive, big-play offense. They won here yesterday with dominant defense. Consider this the start of a new era.

Where once this franchise routinely lost at Three Rivers Stadium to the Pittsburgh Steelers in a number of inventive ways, the Ravens yesterday distanced themselves forever from their Cleveland Browns past.

They did it with an oppressive pass rush, a magnificent goal-line stand and a stifling 16-0 victory over the Steelers in the season opener.

"This is my 11th year, and last year was the first time I won here," said defensive end Rob Burnett, the Ravens' elder statesman. "I can never come here and win. We've gotten to the fourth quarter and lost as the Browns and the Ravens, so this is really sweet."

Defense was clearly the order of the day. If this was a statement game, there was no better place to announce Baltimore's ascension as a dominant defensive force in the AFC than Pittsburgh.

"Everything we do got started here," said defensive coordinator Marvin Lewis, a former Steelers coach and architect of the Ravens' attacking scheme. "There are a lot of reasons why we do what we do. We have respect for the way the Steelers run the ball, the way they play-action pass."

On a day hot enough to curl the toes of cornerback Chris McAlister, the Ravens unloosed a menacing pass rush at Steelers quarterback Kent Graham. Pressured even on quick, three-step drops, Graham absorbed only one sack — that by Burnett — but his 17-for-38 passing performance spoke volumes about the havoc the Ravens raised and the direction they are headed.

"The quarterback stayed on his back the whole entire game," Steelers wide receiver Troy Edwards said of Graham's day.

And there was this from Steelers rookie offensive tackle Marvel Smith: "That was my first game, and they're pretty much the best the NFL has to offer."

The pass rush was so fierce that even when McAlister had to leave the game in the third quarter with cramps from dehydration, the Steelers couldn't capitalize. "My toes were curling up in my shoes," the second-year cornerback said. "Everything below my waist was cramping up."

Not to worry. McAlister returned in time to help blunt the Steelers' biggest scoring threat in the fourth quarter, preserving the shutout. The domination was thorough and complete.

The Ravens didn't surrender a first down until the second quarter. They didn't let the Steelers cross the 50 until the third quarter. They didn't allow a third-down conversion until the third.

If stopping the Steelers' Jerome Bettis was critical, the Ravens succeeded beyond expectations. Bettis ran nine times for 8 yards, the low-water mark of his Steelers' career. The Steelers averaged 1.7 yards per carry on 18 attempts.

Pittsburgh had a collapsing pocket around Graham. No small part of that was due to new defensive tackle Sam Adams.

"I said all along that Sam would help us," Marvin Lewis said. "Having those guys inside who can push the pocket will wear down an offense. That's what you saw at the end."

A defensive stunt by Adams and Burnett led to the Ravens' first points halfway through the first quarter. Adams achieved penetration on a first-down snap at the Pittsburgh 20, and Burnett looped around behind him on a clean, unbroken path to Graham.

Burnett got a sack and a forced fumble, and the Ravens got the ball. Four plays later, Matt Stover kicked the first of three field goals, a 23-yarder.

The Ravens added a 53-yard touchdown pass from quarterback Tony Banks to split end Qadry Ismail three minutes later when the Steelers broke a coverage and allowed Ismail to get behind cornerback Chad Scott. It was Ismail's fourth touchdown of more than 50 yards in two games at Three Rivers.

Other than that, though, it was all defense.

Purple power

GENE SWEENEY JR.

Ravens fans who traveled to Three Rivers Stadium had plenty to cheer about in the season opener.

Sack time

KENNETH K. LAM

Rob Burnett (90) plows into Steelers quarterback Kent Graham, knocking the ball loose as Sam Adams closes. The Ravens recovered the fumble and scored a field goal.

Perhaps the most meaningful was a third-quarter sequence when the Steelers crossed midfield for the first time on a 39-yard pass to Plaxico Burress. After safety Rod Woodson broke up a third-down pass, the Steelers' Kris Brown was wide left on a 45-yard field-goal attempt.

"When they missed the field goal, that pretty much broke their back," Burnett said. "When they couldn't get the three points, I saw their faces and a lot of air come out of them."

The Steelers' best threat came in the form of an 86-yard drive to the Ravens' 1-yard line in the fourth quarter. Graham completed passes of 22, 18 and 22 yards in the drive. After a pass interference penalty against Robert Bailey gave Pittsburgh first-and-goal at the 1, the Steelers inserted Kordell Stewart at quarterback.

Michael McCrary and Adams made plays on first and second down. On third down,

Stewart came away from center without the ball. On fourth down, Stewart exited to boos and Graham re-entered the game, only to throw incomplete out of the end zone. In a game that had already been won, it was another statement. "It meant a lot," Adams said. "It meant we can handle adversity. Regardless of the score, we were able to hold."

"It shows the heart of the defense to allow them to get to the goal line and still keep fighting," said McCrary.

To win on the road was equally significant.

"I've said it before — I think [to win on the road] is the toughest thing to do in all of professional sports," said coach Brian Billick, whose team opens the season with five road games in seven weeks.

Next up is the defending AFC Central champions, the Jacksonville Jaguars, in the Ravens' home opener. McCrary called it "the most important game of the season." It's anther statement waiting to be made.

Hands high

GENE SWEENEY JR.

Ravens cornerback Duane Starks battles the Steelers' Courtney Hawkins for a pass from Kent Graham, causing an incompletion.

7

Clear path

KENNETH K. LAM

Qadry Ismail, having gotten behind the Steelers' Chad Scott, heads to the end zone for a 53-yard touchdown play.

For the defense

KENNETH K. LAM

Rob Burnett celebrates the Ravens' goal-line stand after the defense stopped the Steelers when they had a first down at the 1.

In a rush

Gene Sweeney Jr.

Priest Holmes leaves the Steelers' Mike Vrabel in the AstroTurf while on his way to a 100-yard rushing day.

Strong hit

Kenneth K. Lam

Kim Herring dislodges the ball from the Steelers' Mark Bruener with a hit in the fourth quarter.

GAME 2: Ravens 39, Jaguars 36

September 10, 2000 • PSINet Stadium, Baltimore

Clawing back, Ravens end Jaguars hex

By Ken Murray

If this was their statement game, the Ravens were eloquent yesterday.

If it was a glimpse of the future, they've got a lot to look forward to.

Finding resiliency on defense and a leader on offense, the Ravens dispatched the Jacksonville Jaguars with a raucous 39-36 victory at PSINet Stadium.

On a day when the Ravens finally ended the four-year domination of the Jaguars, they flirted with flashbacks from the past. They fell behind 17-0 in the first quarter, took the lead in the fourth quarter, then relinquished it.

At the end, after the brutal start and torrid comeback, they may finally have become Tony Banks' team.

The Ravens quarterback threw for a career-high five touchdowns and 262 yards. He hit tight end Shannon Sharpe for a 29-yard, game-winning touchdown in the final minute at the end of a 75-yard scoring drive. He wiped out a first half of futility with a second half of wizardry.

Emotions ran rampant all day.

"I've still got that emotion right now," an exhilarated Banks said after completing 23 of 40 throws. "I've won games toward the end, but never in this fashion, by stinking it up in the first half and throwing five touchdown passes. You can't ask for anything more.

"I felt like Kurt Warner."

In the second half, Banks was Kurt Warner, the MVP quarterback of the St. Louis Rams. He passed for four of his five touchdowns and 194 yards after intermission.

"He showed he can take a team over and make the throws necessary to win a game," said Ravens wide receiver Billy Davis. "You don't throw for five touchdown passes and not make a statement."

The victory lifted the 2-0 Ravens into sole possession of the AFC Central Division lead, broke an eight-game losing streak to the Jaguars and stamped them as a team to watch this season.

"They're an outstanding club on both sides of the ball," said Jaguars wide receiver Jimmy Smith, who delivered a Herculean performance with 15 receptions worth 291 yards and three touchdowns. "The only thing they were waiting on was Tony Banks' improvement. He grew a lot today."

Banks grew a lot from the first half to the second.

Three third-down penalties on defense dug a 17-point hole in the first quarter. Jacksonville quarterback Mark Brunell capitalized with a pair of TD throws to Smith for 45 and 43 yards and a 36-yard Mike Hollis field goal.

The Ravens salvaged a 14-yard scoring pass to Travis Taylor after the first of four Jaguars' turnovers. At halftime, Jacksonville led 23-7, and Ravens coach Brian Billick was looking at the big picture.

"At halftime, I told them one thing," Billick said. "What I told them was, win or lose, it will make no difference. The second half will define who we are. How we conduct ourselves will define the kind of team we are."

It took the Ravens four plays to provide the first definition. A series that started with a 40-yard pass to Taylor ended with a 23-yard touchdown strike to the rookie. Taylor had moved from the flanker position to split end when veteran Qadry Ismail sprained a knee ligament returning a Jacksonville kickoff in the first quarter.

Counting Taylor's touchdown, the Ravens outscored the Jaguars 25-3 over 21 minutes as Banks opened up the offense. There was a 5-yard scoring pass to fullback Obafemi Ayanbadejo, a 12-yard touchdown to flanker Jermaine Lewis and a 44-yard field goal by Matt Stover. The field goal was Stover's 22nd consecutive, one away from his personal best.

The Ravens' defense surrendered 386 passing yards to Brunell and five field goals by Hollis. But in the fourth quarter, when the Ravens needed it the most, the defense delivered two huge turnovers.

Linebacker Jamie Sharper provided the first when he knocked the ball loose from Jacksonville running back Stacey Mack, then recovered the fumble himself at the 12. Two plays later, Lewis slipped behind cornerback Fernando Bryant for a 12-yard touchdown catch.

On Jacksonville's next series, safety Corey Harris, subbing for an injured Rod Woodson, deflected a Brunell

Sharpe points

LLOYD FOX

Shannon Sharpe was premature to celebrate this two-point conversion, which was called back by a penalty, but he caught the winning touchdown with less than a minute left.

Dangerous Jaguar

LLOYD FOX

Jimmy Smith gets by Duane Starks and Rod Woodson (26) for his second touchdown. Smith had three on the day.

pass high in the air, and strong safety Kim Herring intercepted.

When Stover converted his 44-yarder, the Ravens held a 32-26 lead. They were merely setting the stage, however.

The Jaguars (1-1) answered with a field goal and a miraculous 40-yard TD catch and run by Smith. With just under two minutes to play, Brunell's third-and-six pass caromed off the hands of wide receiver Keenan McCardell and into Smith's waiting arms.

He ran through a would-be tackle by cornerback Duane Starks — who was victimized on both of Smith's earlier touchdowns — to complete a miracle play.

It was deja vu for the Ravens, but only for a brief while.

With 1:45 left, Banks got the ball on his own 25 and proceeded to take the Ravens down the field. He hit Davis with passes covering 19 and 15 yards. Then he found Ayanbadejo for 12 more.

"It was all business," Ayanbadejo said of the huddle

in that drive. "There wasn't a lot of talk. It was line up and do it. There was like a calm."

Banks spiked the ball with 48 seconds left at the Jacksonville 29. Then, on second down, he rifled a throw deep over the middle to Sharpe, who caught the ball at the 2 and fell forward into the end zone.

An interception by Harris on a fourth-down desperation pass by Brunell ended the game.

The game-winning drive figures to have implications beyond this win.

"Basically, the playoffs run through Tennessee and Jacksonville," Sharpe said, "and we just took a step in the right direction today."

The Ravens seem prepared to take the next step.

"This team is for real for two games," Davis said. "We were able to come through in the clutch in the second half of the second game. If you ask in November, I hope the answer is the same. Now we have to build on this."

Not this time

LLOYD FOX

Tony Banks, who led the Ravens back from a 17-0 deficit, is sacked by the Jaguars' Gary Walker.

Do not pass

LLOYD FOX

Rob Burnett brings down Jaguars quarterback Mark Brunell in the third quarter.

It's over

KARL MERTON FERRON

Coach Brian Billick and offensive linemen Spencer Folau (71) and Edwin Mulitalo cheer the end of the Ravens' futility against the Jaguars.

It's my house

LLOYD FOX

Ray Lewis (next page) fires up himself and the PSINet Stadium crowd upon his introduction at the home opener.

13

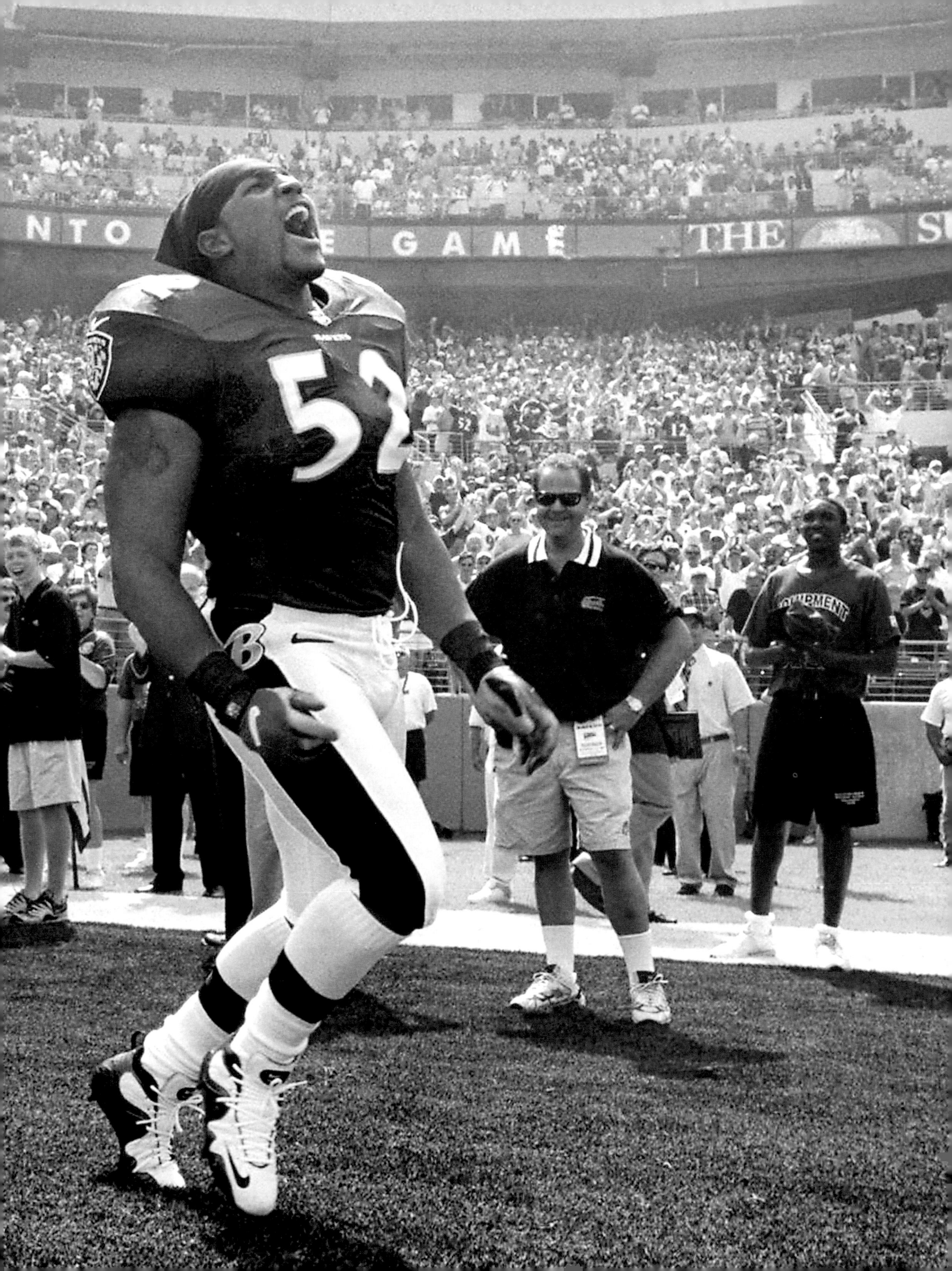

NTO
E GAME
THE
52

Dolphins make sure loss soaks in

By Ken Murray

MIAMI — The Miami Dolphins beat the Ravens at their own game last night. Unleashing a pass rush that sacked quarterback Tony Banks six times — including twice on the goal line — the Dolphins dealt the Ravens a 19-6 dose of reality before 73,464 and a national TV audience at rain-soaked Pro Player Stadium.

It was Miami's defense that dictated in this game and the Dolphins' offense that proved troublesome.

"Every aspect of the game, they physically beat us," Ravens coach Brian Billick said. "It's not about schemes, it's not about coming off an emotionally big win.

"We got physically beat by a very good team. Both sides of the ball — offense and defense — beat us to the punch. There's no explanation, no excuse for it." No short-term relief, either.

The Ravens' first loss of the season dropped them into a three-way tie for the AFC Central Division lead with the Jacksonville Jaguars and the Cleveland Browns at 2-1. "It's going to be a long ride home," Banks said. "I think a lot of us were envisioning ourselves 3-0, playing a home game next week, and that didn't happen. This is another test for us to see how we bounce back from a loss. We haven't lost too much here lately.

"I think we'll be all right. We've got good character people around here. We've just got to get back to work."

A week after the Ravens overturned a 17-0 deficit against the Jaguars to notch an exhilarating win, they spotted the Dolphins (2-1) a 13-point lead and never made up the difference.

The Ravens' offense disappeared in the torrential rains of Hurricane Gordon that pelted the area in the first half, and resurfaced only sporadically in the second. "The weather took a little away from our game," Billick said. "Had it not been raining in the first half, I don't know if it would've changed things."

The Ravens had their chances, however. Altogether, they had four penetrations in the red zone — reaching the 12-, 1-, 15- and 18-yard lines — and all they had to show for it was a pair of Matt Stover field goals. Stover, whose streak of 22 consecutive field goals was broken when his 30-yard attempt at the end of the first half was tipped at the line of scrimmage, hit from 27 and 33 yards.

Baltimore's best opportunity came early in the second half after Lamar Smith punched over for a 7-yard touchdown run for the Dolphins.

From their own 23, the Ravens drove to first-and-goal at the Miami 1 in nine plays. A 6-yard run by fullback Obafemi Ayanbadejo, behind a clearout block by center Jeff Mitchell, carried to the 1.

Over the next three plays, the Ravens had to burn two timeouts and absorbed two critical sacks to back them up to the 10-yard line.

A safety blitz by Brian Walker on first down dropped Banks at the 9. A second-down scramble by Banks got them back to the 3. A third-down sack by Jason Taylor left them staring at a field goal.

Three plays inside the 10. Three aborted pass plays. Billick defended the play calls "because we could not physically shove it in," he said.

Banks accepted blame for the failed pass protection, saying he held the ball too long. Billick spread the blame liberally.

"When it broke down, it was because someone got his ass kicked," he said. "The weather had something to do with it. It was hard to hold onto the ball. We had some miscues. But when there was pressure on the quarterback, someone across the line was getting his ass kicked. There is no other way around it."

The Ravens gave up as many sacks in the first half — four — as they did in the first two games combined. Taylor collected a career-high 2.5 himself.

Not even a handful of big plays from rookie running back Jamal Lewis, who had runs of 45, 17 and 10 yards, could get the Ravens to the end zone.

Banks completed 19 of 31 passes for 189 yards, but fumbled twice and was intercepted at the Miami 4 in the first half when he underthrew wide receiver Patrick Johnson and hit cornerback Patrick Surtain instead.

That gift came two plays after defensive end Rob Burnett caught a

Mud tracks

GENE SWEENEY JR.

The wet conditions in Miami are evident as Chris McAlister (21) knocks down the Dolphins' Oronde Gadsen after a reception.

Out of reach

KARL MERTON
FERRON

Miami's Olindo
Mare kicks over
Keith Washington
(93) for a field
goal in the first
quarter.

Hot pursuit

GENE SWEENEY JR.

Ray Lewis chases Dolphins running back
Lamar Smith, who scored touchdowns on a
run and a pass.

Jay Fiedler pass that clattered off the hands of running back Thurman Thomas and was in the possession briefly of James Trapp.

While Banks struggled with the elements and the Miami pass rush, Fiedler, making his fourth NFL start at quarterback, emerged as a viable performer for the Dolphins.

After hitting just four of nine passes in the first half, Fiedler went 7-for-7 for 121 yards and a touchdown in the second — after the Dolphins staged an elaborate halftime show to retire the jersey of retired quarterback Dan Marino. Fiedler's improvisational 8-yard scoring pass to Smith three plays into the fourth quarter proved huge.

Chased out of the pocket and running to his right, Fiedler flipped a short pass to Smith at the 5, and Smith beat safety Rod Woodson to the goal line.

That touchdown, set up by a 41-yard pass-and-run to tight end Jed Weaver, gave the Dolphins a 19-3 lead. Olindo Mare, who kicked field goals of 42 and 41 yards in the first-half downpour, missed the extra point.

The Ravens came back to get another field goal. Trailing 19-6, they drove to the Miami 18 before a third-down scramble and a fourth-down incompletion by Banks terminated any comeback dream.

"They threw some different stuff at us, but this is the NFL," said left guard Edwin Mulitalo, who recovered one of Banks' fumbles in the first half. "If you can't handle those kinds of things, you don't need to be here. When it came down to it, they got their job done, they got their game plan done, and we didn't."

Billick was succinct in his post-mortem.

"They kicked our ass," he said. "Put it in quotations, put it behind any question you have, and that'll just about answer it."

Kind of a drag

GENE SWEENEY JR.

Ben Coates pulls Dolphins linebacker Derrick Rodgers for a few extra yards on a second-quarter reception.

Not a kick

GENE SWEENEY JR.

Derrick Rodgers (59) has the ball after the Dolphins block a field-goal attempt by Matt Stover, ending his streak of 22 successful kicks.

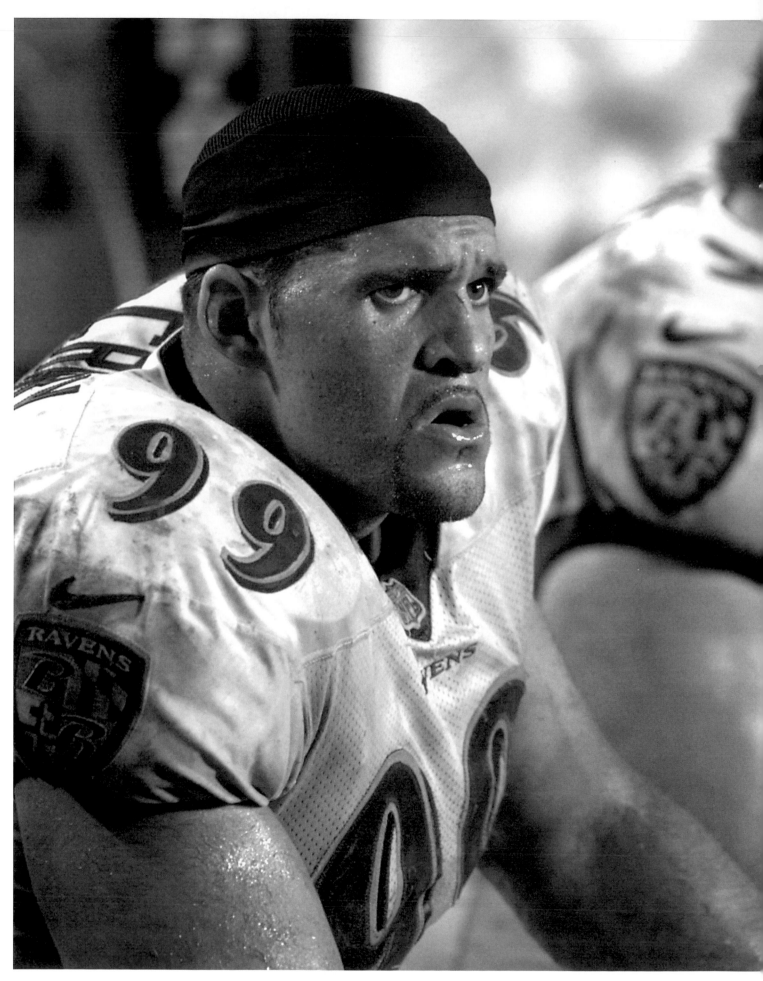

On his back

KARL MERTON FERRON

Jason Taylor tackles
Tony Banks, one of
six Dolphins sacks in
the game and one of
two in goal-to-go
situations.

Feeling soaked

GENE SWEENEY JR.

Michael McCrary
(99) and Tony
Siragusa find no
solace in resting
on the bench after
the Dolphins
score a third-
quarter touch-
down.

No stopping him

DOUG KAPUSTIN

Jamal Lewis runs through the arms
of Takeo Spikes and over Artrell
Hawkins, knocking off his helmet,
for his first NFL touchdown.

Ravens serve up a delicious offensive dish

BY KEN MURRAY

In the fourth week of the season, against the bumbling Cincinnati Bengals, the Ravens found an identity that can take them as far as they want to go.

Integrating smash-mouth football into a diversified offensive profile yesterday, the Ravens drubbed the Bengals, 37-0, at PSINet Stadium before an announced crowd of 68,481.

The Ravens gave Cincinnati a pound of Jamal Lewis, a pinch of Priest Holmes and a ton of defense in a game that essentially was over three plays into the second quarter. When the Bengals lost second-year quarterback Akili Smith on a punishing hit by defensive end Rob Burnett, they were strictly in the survival mode, trailing 17-0. And there was no surviving a defense that established single-game team records for fewest rushing yards (4), passing yards (90), total yards (94) and first downs (seven) allowed.

At 3-1, the Ravens not only regained the AFC Central Division lead — pending tonight's game between Jacksonville and Indianapolis — but they also discovered an offense that can complement their ravenous defense.

"Team is what's going to win ballgames," tight end Shannon Sharpe said. "People keep saying we've got great defense. Well, Tampa has proved you can't win Super Bowls, can't win championships, by playing great defense and not having an offense.

"We're going to take the approach [that] we're going to carry the stick as far as our side of the ball, and let the defense do their thing."

Yesterday, it was Jamal Lewis' stick. The fifth pick of this year's draft debuted as the featured running back with his first NFL touchdown and his first 100-yard game. The touchdown — an 11-yard rumble through three Bengals on the first play of the second quarter — was pure power. The 116-yard game, on 25 carries, was sheer delight for the offensive line.

"You've got to understand what happens when you run the ball," said left guard Edwin Mulitalo. "It just shows dominance. It wears down the defense, we get more confident, and everything works out the way you want."

The Ravens ran the Bengals (0-3) into the ground. When it wasn't Lewis, it was Holmes, who gave up his lead job this week, but not his big plays. Holmes dashed for 51 yards on eight carries, and caught four passes for 48 more, barely missing a 100-yard game of his own.

Altogether, the Ravens rushed for 176 yards, averaging 4.6 a carry, which balanced out quarterback Tony Banks' 196-yard, two-touchdown passing game.

"What was really nice was the one-two punch of Priest and Jamal," coach Brian Billick said. "Priest is being just an ultimate professional coming in, doing what he can, helping in the locker room before the game. He's just coaching like a son of a gun with Jamal, taking the little points of what he needs to do."

Holmes spent most of the week, and a large part of the game, talking Lewis through the job. The team's running backs meet at Lewis' home on Thursday nights — the rookie picks up the dinner tab — to share information.

"We watch film on Thursday nights, and all week he tells me to be patient," Lewis said, "because he knows I have a tendency to just get worked up and want to hit it fast." Lewis' impact on offense wasn't only in the extra yards he punched out. It was also seen in ball control.

"He gives us time of possession," said Sharpe, whose 1-yard touchdown catch opened a 24-0 lead in the second quarter. "He keeps our offense on the field. He and Priest have contrasting running styles. He's more of a banger, and still can take it the distance. Priest is more of a slasher who makes people miss. One thing they do have in common — they're both very effective."

The running game helped the Ravens amass a whopping 17-minute edge in time of possession, and the passing game benefited. The Ravens converted 11 of their first 13 third downs. Banks, who had struggled on third downs, threw 11 of his 20 completions on third down.

"I threw good balls and we caught 'em," Banks said. "Pretty simple."

Banks threw an 8-yard scoring pass to rookie flanker Travis Taylor on third down for a 10-0, first-quarter

Power back

Jamal Lewis served notice of his arrival in the NFL with a 116-yard effort against the Bengals.

lead. It came on the same play that Taylor dropped earlier in the quarter, a quick slant.

When Billick had backup quarterback Chris Redman still throwing to Taylor late in the fourth quarter, it heated up a rivalry in which the Ravens have beaten the Bengals five straight times.

Taylor caught two passes in a 40-yard drive that started with 5:27 left in the game. When officials ruled Taylor down outside the goal line on the second one, with two minutes left, Billick challenged the call and lost. The Ravens settled for a 19-yard Matt Stover field goal.

The upshot was that Bengals coach Bruce Coslet left the field abruptly at game's end without the traditional post-game handshake with Billick.

While Coslet issued only a terse post-game comment and took no questions, it was left to his players to address the ill will.

"That's something that is disappointing to see and when you're on the other side of it, it really makes you mad," said former Ravens quarterback Scott Mitchell, who coughed up three turnovers after replacing Smith. "I'm sure it's something that we won't forget."

Linebacker Steve Foley was even more agitated.

"Division opponents, some kind of rivalry, I don't know," he said. "That's how it is for a lot of teams. Some of them try to pay you some respect; others don't.

"Next time we play these [players], we need to hit them in their mouth like they did us, so at the end of the game they're not wanting to shake our hands. That's how it's going to be."

Flying Raven

Priest Holmes tries to leap through the tackle of Takeo Spikes during the first quarter. Holmes' rushing and receiving totaled 99 yards.

Forget it

Kenneth K. Lam

Rob Burnett and Ray
Lewis (52) team to stop
Corey Dillon behind the
line. The Ravens
allowed the Bengals
only 4 yards rushing.

That's the way

DOUG KAPUSTIN

Rob Burnett (left) makes his point after sacking Akili Smith, knocking the Bengals quarterback out of the game.

Holding on

DOUG KAPUSTIN

Jermaine Lewis manages to catch this pass from Tony Banks during the fourth quarter. The Ravens kept passing when the game had long been decided, angering the Bengals.

Defense adds a blank page to history book

By Ken Murray

CLEVELAND — Brian Billick tossed out the bait last week and his defense snatched it up like another unprotected football.

Looking to the history books for their motivation, the Ravens smothered the Cleveland Browns with their second straight shutout and third of the young season yesterday.

The 12-0 victory before a paid crowd of 73,018 at Cleveland Browns Stadium was less about art than realism. And reality said the hottest defense in the NFL is setting standards that will be hard to match.

History? The last team that threw back-to-back shutouts was the 1985 Chicago Bears. The last team that collected three shutouts in one season was the 1991 Washington Redskins.

Bottom line: Both teams won Super Bowls.

Billick, the Ravens' full-time psychologist and part-time historian, didn't miss his chance.

"We threw that out to our guys as a challenge," the Ravens coach said of the 15-year drought in back-to-back shutouts. "And that is no disrespect to the Browns. It didn't matter who we were coming in against."

The Ravens have two road wins this season and both are shutouts. They have won seven straight games against AFC Central Division opponents. They haven't allowed a touchdown in more than 133 minutes, dating to early in the fourth quarter of their loss in Miami. At 4-1, they enjoy the best start of their short Baltimore tenure.

In this case at least, domination starts with defense.

"Every NFL team has a $62 million salary cap," said defensive end Rob Burnett. "We're shutting them out, the best of the best, every week. We play the best available athletes money can buy.

"To be able to get a shutout in this league is phenomenal."

The Ravens have three shutouts in five games this season, four in their past seven. With Matt Stover kicking four field goals, they preserved yesterday's shutout with four turnovers and a resiliency in the red zone.

They were creative beyond conventional means. When the Browns (2-3) set up at the Baltimore 8 after a 38-yard pass from quarterback Tim Couch to David Patten in the second quarter, defensive back Robert Bailey forced Marc Edwards to fumble on consecutive plays.

The first came on a short pass at the 4, and Edwards fell on his own fumble. On the next play, the Browns ran Edwards up the middle, and the blitzing Bailey stripped the ball. That was recovered by Ravens safety Rod Woodson in the end zone.

"On the first one, I tried to hit him and drive my arms inside, and the ball came out," said Bailey, a free-agent addition in the off-season. "But it bounced right back to him. The second one, he was holding the ball on his side and I just jumped on him and swiped at his hand, and the ball came out."

Twice in the fourth quarter, the Browns drove inside the Ravens' 20, only to be denied the end zone. Ray Lewis' interception on a ball thrown right at his chest at the 15 snuffed one Cleveland threat. And a fourth-down tackle by nickel back James Trapp on a short pass to rookie back Travis Prentice finished it off.

Yes, the Ravens took the shutout bait. For the record, those 1985 Bears beat Dallas, 44-0, on Nov. 17, and Atlanta, 36-0, a week later.

"We talked about it all week," Bailey said. "We talked about it on the field. We talked about it when we were in the red zone.

"Basically, I was saying to the guys, 'This is the red zone, this is what we're all about. Let's not let them in, let's get the ball.' That's what happened."

In the city that made the Dawg Pound fashionable, Woodson made an appropriate canine analogy about the Ravens' red zone success.

"You see those dogs when they're getting chased and their hair raises up," Woodson said. "It's like, 'I've got my house here, I've got to fight a little bit.'

"I think when they get down there, we get a little more aggressive. I think our character and pride come into play, and we play a little harder, a little more focused." Lewis described the atmosphere in the red zone in simpler

One-man gang

DOUG KAPUSTIN

Four Browns converge on Jamal Lewis, who doesn't go down easily.

Going the other way

KENNETH K. LAM

Ray Lewis clutches an interception as the Browns' Dennis Northcutt tries to get the ball back. The turnover ended a scoring threat at the 15.

terms.

"It's gut-check time," he said, "and we look each other in the eyes and say somebody's got to make a play."

A week after the Ravens ravaged the Cincinnati Bengals for four touchdowns and 37 points, their offense sputtered against the Browns' injury-depleted defense.

"We had as many mental errors in the first half as we've had since I've been here," said quarterback Tony Banks, who completed 18 of 34 throws for 169 yards and one interception. "We didn't have that passion.

"We didn't attack with the run the way maybe we should have with their injury situation."

The Browns were without starting linebacker Rahim Abdullah and his backup, Lenoy Jones. The Ravens balanced the scale by playing two backup tackles in the second half after Harry Swayne and Jonathan Ogden went out with sprained ankles.

After rushing for 81 yards in the first half, the Ravens rushed for 107 in the second. Rookie Jamal Lewis led the team with 86 yards, but played sparingly after halftime because of a hip pointer. Priest Holmes picked up the slack and gained 68 of his 82 yards in the second half.

"I was very gratified by the physical play in the second half," Billick said. He was more gratified by his defense, which he described as "magnificent." The shutout talk was the right touch.

"We have to get motivated somehow," Burnett said. "What better motivation than to be in the record books. I think it worked."

Even as the words Super Bowl have crept more and more into the Ravens' vocabulary, Burnett was cautiously optimistic.

"I'm not going to start blowing smoke, or make predictions, or print Super Bowl tickets yet," he said. "But so far, so good."

Out of pocket

KENNETH K. LAM

The Browns' Marquis Smith gets to quarterback Tony Banks for a loss during the second quarter.

No-score zone

DOUG KAPUSTIN

Rod Woodson recovers Marc Edwards' fumble in the end zone, halting a Browns scoring threat. Robert Bailey knocked the ball loose.

31

Hang on

KENNETH K. LAM

James Trapp pulls down the Browns' Kevin Johnson on a fourth-quarter reception.

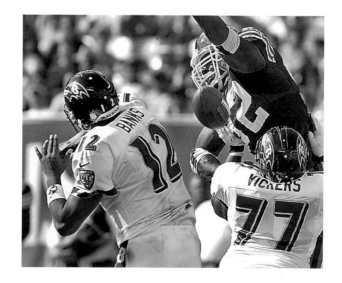

Off-target

DOUG KAPUSTIN

The defense recorded a shutout, but the Ravens' offense wasn't clicking, as evidenced by Corey Fuller's interception of this pass intended for Jermaine Lewis.

Brown block

DOUG KAPUSTIN

Cleveland's Courtney Brown knocks down a pass by Tony Banks.

No offense, but victory is still a kick

BY MIKE PRESTON

JACKSONVILLE, Fla. — Here is a summary of one of the Ravens' scoring drives last night: four plays, minus-1 yard, elapsed time of 1 minute and 35 seconds. That one ended with a 33-yard field goal from Matt Stover.

Here was another: three plays, minus-3 yards, elapsed time of 1:11, which resulted in a 24-yard field goal.

Almost every Ravens scoring drive these days ends with a Stover field goal. Stover had a career-high five last night in the Ravens' 15-10 victory over the Jacksonville Jaguars at ALLTEL Stadium.

The optimistic Ravens fans are glad the team is 5-1 and atop the AFC Comedy Central and that defending champion Jacksonville (2-4) has almost no shot at winning the division title or possibly gaining a playoff bid.

But when your field-goal kicker is your best offensive weapon and your team's best pass catcher is the fullback, you have problems.

And, oh my, do the Ravens have offensive problems. Thank goodness they have a good defense.

Up until the fourth quarter last night, the Ravens' defense hadn't allowed a touchdown in eight quarters, but their offense hasn't scored one in that time either, going back to the fourth quarter of the Bengals game with 6:39 remaining.

Everyone knew it would take time for the offense to develop with new players such as tight ends Shannon Sharpe and Ben Coates, running back Jamal Lewis and receiver Travis Taylor, but time is winding down.

There has been no progress in the past two weeks. Last week, the Ravens needed four field goals from Stover for a 12-0 win against the Cleveland Browns.

It's not that the Ravens can't score points — they can't even use up the clock. Ahead 15-10 last night with 3:50 remaining in the game, the Ravens' offense used 66 seconds. The Ravens had only 193 yards of total offense last night and converted on only three of 17 third-down situations. Quarterback Tony Banks completed 17 of 39 passes for 154 yards and the team averaged just 2.3 yards a carry.

It's time to get a little concerned. It's time for owner Art Modell to call the complex to ask coach Brian Billick and team vice president Ozzie Newsome what's going on. Eventually, especially if the Ravens make the playoffs, they are going to have to score some points. The Ravens cannot live on Stover alone.

Billick said last night that after such an emotional win, there wasn't time to worry about such things as third-down conversions and red-zone effectiveness. OK, but somebody has to take the blame. You can start with Billick, quarterback Tony Banks, the offensive line. Point at the receivers, too. It's a mess.

The unit has no consistency or identity, starting with the play-calling. The Ravens can't decide if they are a passing team or a running team. Last night, they weren't successful at either one. The team's best offensive play this year is a swing pass to fullback Obafemi Ayanbadejo in the flat out of the backfield. Sound familiar, straight out of the Ted Marchibroda play book?

As for Banks, he is developing, but with baby-step progression. His major improvements are that he no longer throws into coverage and he takes better care of handling the football.

But he is such a streaky quarterback. He has to find a rhythm and release the ball quickly or he is off target. When Banks has to hold onto the ball, that's when he has trouble.

Last night, when he had time to throw, Banks either threw high or behind a lot of his receivers. That sling-shot throwing motion of his, similar to that of Randall Cunningham's, allows for a number of passes to be knocked down.

There were also a lot of times Banks couldn't throw. The Ravens' offensive line has been depleted by injuries, and the unit had problems picking up Jacksonville's blitzes. The Ravens were without Pro Bowl offensive left tackle Jonathan Ogden last night, out with a severely sprained ankle. The team also lost starting center Jeff Mitchell with an ankle injury for the game with 2:44 remaining in the first quarter.

Mitchell's absence forced right guard Mike Flynn to move to center,

Leave him hanging

GENE SWEENEY JR.

Tony Banks tries to get away to pass with the Jaguars' Gary Walker on his back. Behind a depleted offensive line, Banks faced lots of pressure.

Wrong receiver

GENE SWEENEY JR.

Chris McAlister waits on an overthrown pass, intended for Jimmy Smith, that he intercepts to end the Jaguars' last drive with a minute left in the game.

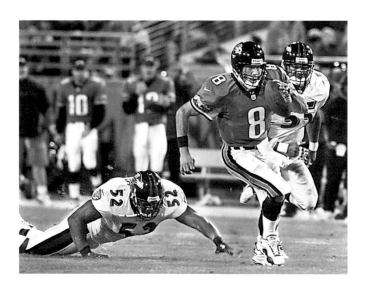

On the run

GENE SWEENEY JR.

Jaguars quarterback Mark Brunell escapes Ray Lewis (52) and Jamie Sharper, but the Ravens harassed him most of the game.

and Orlando Bobo was inserted at guard. One could see a timing problem within the group. But Banks and the receivers should have had enough time to work out a lot of their problems.

Yet Sharpe is still having problems learning the offense. Third-year receiver Patrick Johnson, possibly the fastest guy on the team, has disappeared. Backup tight end Coates is just a blocker. The only two receivers who show up regularly are Qadry Ismail and Taylor, and neither one of them has been effective in the red zone, where the Ravens are one of the least productive teams in the NFL.

The Ravens' defense bailed them out again last night as cornerback Chris McAlister picked off a Jamie Martin pass with about a minute remaining, but the defense can't hold up forever.

Sooner or later, the offense will have to show up.

"It's a huge win," said Banks. "We would have liked the offense to play better, and anytime they turn the ball over six times, you like to get more than 15 points out of it. But like I told our defense, it's an honor playing with those guys. There has been games where we have bailed them out.

"But the last couple of weeks, they've been bailing us out," Banks added. "Our defense is incredible, and I'm glad I don't have to play against them. We can't be a championship-caliber team if we don't score more than 15 points on six turnovers."

Point man

GENE SWEENEY JR.

Matt Stover celebrates one of his five field goals. With the Ravens stalling on offense, Stover provided all of the points in the victory over Jacksonville.

Broken up

KARL MERTON FERRON

The Jaguars' Kevin Hardy (51) knocks away a potential touchdown catch by Shannon Sharpe.

Defense never rests

Karl Merton Ferron

Lional Dalton (91) and Ray Lewis congratulate Kim Herring for his fourth-quarter interception.

GAME 7: Redskins 10, Ravens 3

October 15, 2000 • FedEx Field, Landover, Md.

With red light in red zone, Ravens stall

BY KEN MURRAY

LANDOVER — The road trip finally ended for the Ravens yesterday, but the drought didn't.

One more time, the red zone turned into the Bermuda Triangle. One more time, the end zone was a forbidden paradise. One more time, quarterback Tony Banks was left to explain how all those high-priced offensive weapons disappeared under a cloud of mistakes.

And there was no explaining a 10-3 loss to the Washington Redskins before 83,252 at FedEx Field.

It was a game that boiled down to two plays — one that Redskins running back Stephen Davis made and one that Banks didn't.

When Davis ran through a gaping hole on the right side of the Ravens' defensive line — and through safety Rod Woodson — early in the fourth quarter for a 33-yard touchdown, the Ravens (5-2) relinquished their hold on first place in the AFC Central Division.

When Banks threw an interception on the goal line at the end of the first half, it sent the offense spiraling toward its third straight performance — all road games — without a touchdown.

The Ravens haven't reached the end zone since the fourth quarter of a Sept. 24 rout of the Cincinnati Bengals. The drought spans 13 quarters, 186 minutes, 39 seconds of clock time and 36 possessions. It's the longest current dry spell in the NFL.

More? The Ravens have scored one touchdown in five road games this season, none in the past four.

"This here is ridiculous," said tight end Shannon Sharpe, one of the Ravens' expensive off-season additions. "I'm very disappointed. I just told Tony, 'You're going to get all the blame, and you have to understand that. But you can't get down on yourself.'"

The Ravens acknowledged confusion on a stunt call that opened the gate for Davis' touchdown run. Banks' mistake was much more obvious, and painful. But the end-of-the-half sequence was hardly all his fault. Poor clock management was also a contributing factor.

The Ravens got the ball with 2:57 left in the first half when linebacker Jamie Sharper forced a Davis fumble and cornerback Chris McAlister recovered at the Redskins' 42.

After Banks ad-libbed a 10-yard run, running back Jamal Lewis got the call on the next four plays to reach the 10-yard line, where the Ravens called their first timeout with 56 seconds left. They got just two plays off in the next 46 seconds, though. There was a 2-yard loss for Lewis, then a pass-interference call against Washington's Matt Stevens in the end zone.

On first-and-goal from the 1 with 10 seconds left, Banks threw over the middle for Sharpe, but found linebacker Kevin Mitchell instead for a drive-killing interception, the first of Mitchell's six-year career.

Billick said he eschewed a run because of the amount of time left.

The play sent in was a pass to wide receiver Travis Taylor, who was covered. Sharpe was the third read, a "last resort," Sharpe said.

"I saw [Sharpe], and I thought I had a little seam, but obviously I didn't. Coach [Billick] tells me constantly not to throw a flat ball down there, and I threw a flat ball," Banks said.

Banks, in fact, threw the ball over the middle late and low. H-back Obafemi Ayanbadejo came open late when linebacker Shawn Barber peeled off him to help make a play against Sharpe.

In despair, left tackle Jonathan Ogden, playing with a sprained right ankle, yanked his helmet off, threw it, then kicked it.

The frustration of three straight touchdown-less weeks on the road had bubbled to the surface.

"That ain't nothing new," Ogden said of his helmet-throwing fit.

Neither was it a sign, he said, that he was frustrated with his quarterback.

"No, everyone plays a part," Ogden said. "It's not one person. We have to block better, run better, catch better."

Billick, meanwhile, did not waver in his support for Banks.

"Tony Banks is my starting quarterback, without question," he said.

Why? "Because he's the starting quarterback, we're a 5-2 team, and that's the guy I think gives us the best chance to win right now."

Bat man

GENE SWEENEY JR.

Duane Starks stops a potential touchdown by batting away a pass from the Redskins' Albert Connell.

Not this time

LLOYD FOX

Corey Harris pounds Andre Reed, preventing a Redskins completion.

For the third consecutive week, Banks' passing yardage dropped. Against Washington, he was 16-for-27 for 135 yards.

Yesterday, Banks said the offensive woes were getting to him.

"I feel I'm pressing out there," he said. "I threw balls into the dirt that I never have. I've got to relax. I think coming into today, I wanted to put it all on my shoulders. I wanted to make plays downfield. That didn't happen early, and I started pressing even more."

Banks missed a potential 62-yard touchdown pass in the first quarter, when Redskins cornerback Darrell Green strained his right calf trying to cover wide-out Jermaine Lewis. But Banks' deep throw sent the wide-open Lewis out of bounds at the Redskins' 30 to make a non-catch.

The only scoring the Ravens achieved was a 51-yard field goal by reliable Matt Stover in the second quarter, after rookie Kris Heppner hit a 37-yarder for the Redskins (5-2). Stover has scored the Ravens' last 34 points.

The Ravens are 0-for-14 in the red zone in their five road games.

"It's weird," said split end Qadry Ismail. "I don't feel like we're getting a return on our investment. [But] we really, really are solid with each other. To not show up on game day, it's kind of an enigma."

Even the Ravens' defense succumbed in the second half, when Davis rushed for 89 of his game-high 91 yards. Davis' running and a suspect illegal contact penalty on safety Kim Herring allowed the Redskins to run out the last 5:30 of the game. Herring was called for bumping tight end Stephen Alexander on a pass that sailed over the Redskins' bench.

"It was a bad call," Herring said. "You make a call like that, when the ball is five yards out of bounds ... you don't make that kind of call in that kind of situation this late in the game."

The Ravens finished the five-road-games-in-seven-weeks portion of their schedule with a better-than-expected 5-2 record, but in a major offensive drought.

"I don't care how good your defense is, you can't win like that," Sharpe said. "It'll catch up with you. It caught up with us today."

Daylight

GENE SWEENEY JR.

Priest Holmes finds a hole to run for a first down, leaping over Sam Shade.

42

No cracks

KARL MERTON FERRON

Jamal Lewis, met by a wall of Redskins defenders, was just part of a Ravens offense that wasn't producing against Washington.

What to do?

GENE SWEENEY JR.

Neither Brian Billick nor receiver Patrick Johnson can figure out what to do on a third-and-24 in the fourth quarter.

Score stopper

KARL MERTON FERRON

On a play from the Washington 1 with 10 seconds left in the first half, the Redskins' Kevin Mitchell steps in front of Shannon Sharpe to intercept a pass.

Frustration

LLOYD FOX

Even from the back, the wear of the Ravens' touchdown drought shows on quarterback Tony Banks as he leaves the field with a loss.

GAME 8: Titans 14, Ravens 6

October 22, 2000 • PSINet Stadium, Baltimore

Out of luck, still out of end zone

BY KEN MURRAY

This is what October has come to for the Ravens: On the 1-yard line, quarterback Tony Banks produced a fumble when he should have had a touchdown. On the 9-yard line, Tennessee Titans quarterback Steve McNair produced a touchdown when he should have been sacked.

There were no reprieves for the Ravens at PSINet Stadium yesterday in an excruciating, 14-6 loss to the Titans before a record crowd of 69,200.

Not in the red zone. Not in the replay challenge system. Not in sheer dumb luck.

Ravens coach Brian Billick, shut out of the end zone since Sept. 24, finally went to his bench for veteran quarterback Trent Dilfer, and came away with a replay headache. In three fourth-quarter possessions, Dilfer delivered a punt, an interception and a controversy when his tantalizing fourth-down pass to Qadry Ismail looked, upon further review, reasonably close to a 33-yard touchdown.

But like every other critical play near the goal line yesterday, the Ravens lost the replay challenge.

"It wasn't inconclusive," Ismail said insistently. "Both feet were in, and the momentum of the defender ... if he had not pushed me, I would've been in. That's my story. I'm sticking by it."

The Ravens' story has gone from bad to worse. At 5-3, they're a tenuous second in the AFC Central race, a half-game ahead of the Pittsburgh Steelers, who come to PSINet next week, and 1½ games behind the Titans.

Worse? The Ravens' offense is a mess. For the fourth consecutive game, it failed to score a touchdown. The grim count now is 16 quarters, 49 possessions and 246 minutes, 39 seconds of clock time.

Banks hasn't thrown a touchdown pass in 17 quarters, and may not anytime soon if Billick decides Dilfer gives the Ravens a better chance to beat the Steelers.

Banks was pulled after throwing three interceptions in four third-quarter possessions. Two went to middle linebacker Randall Godfrey. One, Godfrey returned for a 24-yard touchdown.

When Banks missed wide receiver Travis Taylor in the end zone — but found Titans cornerback Dainon Sidney instead — Billick had seen enough.

"I just thought it was the right time to do it," Billick said. "I didn't think the things that happened to him [in the first half] warranted him being pulled out at that time."

Despite protecting Banks through the drought, Billick now has a full-scale quarterback controversy on his hands. He wouldn't announce next week's starter, and may not until kickoff.

The decision, he said, will be based on "where we are as a team, who can get the job done against the opponent we're playing. There are a lot of factors involved."

Banks had his moments, however. He completed 17 of 32 passes for 229 yards — his highest yardage total in six weeks. He completed six passes for 20 yards or more. But on one of the game's biggest plays, he mishandled the snap from backup center Mike Flynn, playing for injured Jeff Mitchell, with the Ravens threatening at the Tennessee 1 in the first quarter.

From first-and-goal at the 3, two runs put the Ravens at the 1. Banks came away from center without the ball, recovered the fumble at the 3, and the Ravens settled for a 21-yard field goal by Matt Stover.

"Me and Mike didn't get the snap," Banks said. "That's something we've got to work on."

"Maybe I didn't bring it up too fast," said Flynn. "It's hard to say."

The Ravens drove 77 yards on their next possession, leading to a 38-yard field goal from Stover, who has scored the team's last 40 points. The psychological impact of failing to reach the end zone is growing.

"It's like a hex on us at the goal line now," said right tackle Harry Swayne, who battled Tennessee's Jevon Kearse to a standstill. "It's like spirits come down to spook on us. They say, °Not today.'

"It's almost like it's unbelievable. We know we can get down there. When we get down there, it's like, °What could it be now to keep us out?'

"Most of the time, it's us."

47

Can't grasp it

LLOYD FOX

If Travis Taylor could have held on to this pass while Denard Walker defended, the Ravens would have had a touchdown.

The Ravens won the battle of statistics, but lost the war of attrition to a team that started the game without its best cornerback (Samari Rolle) and one of its top receivers (Carl Pickens). The Titans also lost running back Eddie George to a sprained medial collateral knee ligament after one play.

But Tennessee still had the magic of McNair, who turned in a devilish play at the end of the first half to capture a 7-6 lead.

The Titans got their opportunity after a 29-yard punt return by Derrick Mason to the Baltimore 38. In four plays, they were at the 9-yard line, facing third-and-five. Then, under pressure, McNair pirouetted out of the grasp of defensive end Rob Burnett and threw across his body to Rodney Thomas, George's replacement. Thomas bolted into the end zone, and the Titans never relinquished the lead.

Not even a miraculous return by defen-sive tackle Tony Siragusa was enough on this day. Siragusa suffered a bruised spinal cord in the first quarter, and had to be immobilized and carried off the field. But after X-rays and a magnetic resonance imaging exam at the nearby Maryland Shock Trauma Center, he was cleared to return. He was on the field for McNair's touchdown pass and played extensively in the second half.

"For him to come back like that shows such guts and character," said Ismail.

Ismail's last-gasp attempt at Dilfer's long pass in the final two minutes served as the punctuation mark on a day of utter frustration. After he and cornerback Michael Booker went up for the ball, Ismail got his left foot down in bounds and appeared to drag his right foot on the end line.

"To me, if the second foot being in was at all debatable, then the idea that he was forced out via contact should have been a slam-dunk decision," said Billick.

Faring no better

LLOYD FOX

Trent Dilfer, being sacked
by Jason Fisk, came in for
Tony Banks, but couldn't
produce a victory.

Benched

KENNETH K. LAM

Tony Banks is
consoled after his
three-intercep-
tion performance
in the third quar-
ter landed him on
the bench.

Scrambler

John Makely

Steve McNair's agility
frustrates the Ravens
again, as the Titans
quarterback runs for a
first down.

Taking it back

LLOYD FOX

Randall Godfrey intercepts a pass by Tony Banks and runs it in for a touchdown. Godfrey had two interceptions on the day.

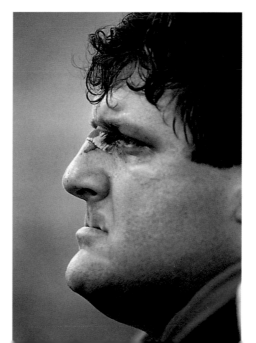

'Goose' down

JOHN MAKELY

Tony Siragusa watches the last seconds tick off in the Titans' victory. He had returned to the game after suffering a bruised spinal cord.

GAME 9: Steelers 9, Ravens 6

October 29, 2000 • PSINet Stadium, Baltimore

End zone, playoffs look far away

BY KEN MURRAY

Second place is gone.
Home-field advantage is debatable.
The playoffs, at this moment, look like a pipe dream.
The Ravens' free fall through the AFC Central continued yesterday with a wretched 9-6 loss to the Pittsburgh Steelers in front of 69,405, the largest crowd in PSINet Stadium history.

Undone by another desultory offensive performance, the Ravens lost their third straight game and landed with a thud in third place at 5-4.

After five consecutive games without a touchdown, how much more embarrassment can one offense endure?

"The perspective here has to change," Ravens coach Brian Billick said grimly, after losing his second straight home game. "There are no easy answers for this. We're in a dead dogfight now to reach our main objective, which is to reach the playoffs."

Playoffs? The Ravens would be ecstatic just to reach the end zone these days.

Not even a change in quarterbacks could get them there yesterday. A recharged running game didn't do it, either. And perhaps worst of all, even the Ravens' superb kicking game couldn't pull the trigger when it had a chance in the fourth quarter.

Quarterback Trent Dilfer, making his first start in 11 months, replaced Tony Banks with almost predictable results. He completed 11 of 24 passes for 152 yards, but committed two critical turnovers — one a fumble on the Steelers' 9-yard line, the other an interception in the end zone.

Rookie running back Jamal Lewis got the ball 22 times and accounted for 146 of the team's 274 yards from scrimmage, 93 of them rushing. He had a 35-yard run and a 40-yard catch-and-run, and still the Ravens couldn't find the end zone.

The touchdown drought is approaching mythic proportions. The Ravens haven't gotten to the end zone in 20 quarters, 58 possessions and a staggering 306 minutes, 39 seconds. They haven't scored a touchdown since Obafemi Ayanbadejo plunged in from the 1 on Sept. 24 in the fourth quarter of a 37-0 rout of the Cincinnati Bengals.

Their touchdown-less October placed the Ravens in some not-so-elite company. The 1993 Indianapolis Colts went 20 quarters without a touchdown; the 1991 Colts went 21.

"You can't call it a dry spell anymore," said center Jeff Mitchell.

It's full-scale retreat, with angst.

"Sometimes I wish I was a billionaire," said millionaire tight end Shannon Sharpe, "because I'd like to give the fans all their money back, because this is ridiculous. They deserve to have their money back the way we played in the past [month]."

That's a check owner Art Modell won't write. He's already spent enough on an offense that can't score.

The Ravens' latest debacle featured two puzzling special teams plays. A fumbled kickoff by Corey Harris led to Kris Brown's winning 24-yard field goal in the third quarter. Billick lost a replay challenge — and a vital timeout — trying to get the ball back.

But the bigger curiosity came in the fourth quarter, with the Steelers up 9-6 and the Ravens with the ball on the Pittsburgh 33. Rather than attempt a tying 50-yard field goal on fourth-and-six or try for the first down, Billick opted to punt with less than eight minutes left.

He was hoping to pin the Steelers deep, then get the ball back for his offense in good field position. The strategy backfired, however, when the Steelers ran the next 4:46 off the clock and pinned the Ravens on their 10 with a punt.

Kicking with the 20-mph wind gusts, Matt Stover had already hit from 51 and 49 yards in the second quarter, extending his streak of consecutive points to 46. In the fourth quarter, the Ravens went into the wind.

"Matt felt it was outside his range," Billick said. "We have reached a pretty good comfort zone about communicating with one another about the distance, the wind, whatever."

Stover said he maintained a constant conversation with offensive coordinator Matt Cavanaugh and special teams coach Russ Purnell about field conditions in the fourth quarter.

"The field conditions weren't very good, either," Stover said. "Everything

No connection

Doug Kapustin

Qadry Ismail and the Steelers' Dewayne Washington battle for a pass that falls incomplete.

53

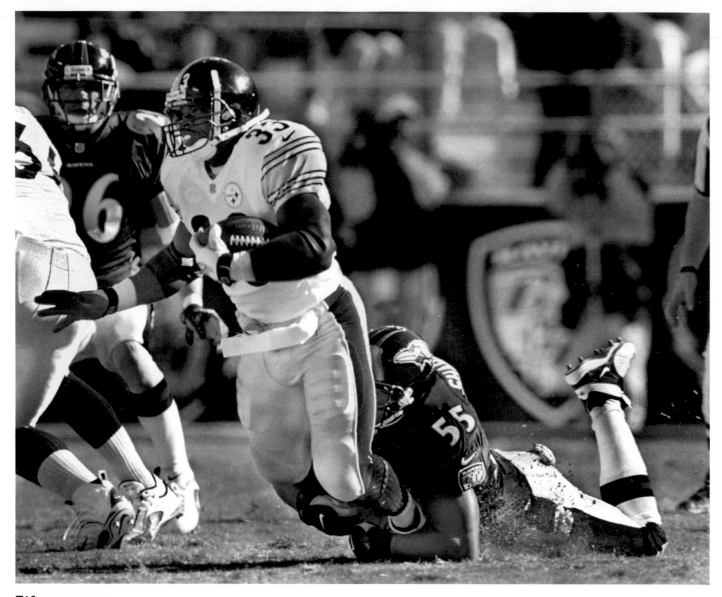

It's a wrap

LLOYD FOX

Jamie Sharper locks on the legs of Steelers running back Richard Huntley.

Air Dilfer

DOUG KAPUSTIN

Trent Dilfer (right) dives for a first down on an opening drive that would end in a turnover.

had to be pretty much perfect in that situation, and they weren't. I said, 'You've got to get me to the 30-, 32-yard line.' It was the 33. It didn't work out.

"If I missed it, I didn't want them to get the ball on the 41-, 42-yard line. As it ended up, they got the ball on the 10."

A defense that has allowed just four touchdowns in the past six games gave up one too many yesterday. That was a 45-yard pass from Kordell Stewart to Hines Ward that left cornerback Duane Starks clutching at another big play.

Stewart, 6-0 against the Ravens, ran a bootleg and Hines ran a streak pattern. Starks said Hines normally runs a deep out when Stewart runs a bootleg.

The Ravens didn't make the two big plays on offense that could have gotten them out of the drought, either. Dilfer simply mishandled Mitchell's snap after driving to the Pittsburgh 9 on his first series.

In the third quarter, he was intercepted by cornerback Dewayne Washington when he overthrew split end Qadry Ismail.

"I threw the ball a little late," Dilfer said. "Interceptions are part of the game. If you're afraid to throw the ball up in a position where a guy can make a play, then you've got no future as a quarterback."

In the fourth quarter, the Ravens lost rookie flanker Travis Taylor with a broken left collarbone, an injury suffered when he dropped a high pass. He's expected to miss four to six weeks.

"You can't go out there and play not to lose," said safety Rod Woodson. "You've got to go out there and play to win. And I don't know that we've done that these last three weeks, to be honest."

Let the dogfight begin. Next week, the Ravens visit Cincinnati.

Up the ladder

DOUG KAPUSTIN

Hines Ward leaps over
the Ravens' Duane
Starks for a 45-yard
touchdown pass.

Staring at a loss

LLOYD FOX

Duane Starks absorbs the
realization that the Ravens
have dropped to 5-4.

Ridden down

LLOYD FOX

Trent Dilfer, being
sacked by Joey Porter,
didn't meet with much
success in his first start.

November 5, 2000 • Paul Brown Stadium, Cincinnati

Back in the end zone, back on track

BY KEN MURRAY

CINCINNATI — Quarterback Trent Dilfer danced in front of the Ravens' bench, index fingers shooting flares into the sky.

Split end Qadry Ismail and guard Edwin Mulitalo lifted the Ravens' unlikeliest hero, Brandon Stokley, above the gathering crowd in the end zone.

Coach Brian Billick, along the side-line, rammed both arms into the air to acknowledge the long-awaited touchdown.

When Stokley, a second-year wide receiver, turned a soft toss from Dilfer into an electric, 14-yard touchdown pass in the second quarter, it ended the NFL's longest touchdown drought since the 1974 Chicago Bears went 22 quarters without one.

Better yet for the Ravens, it sent them cartwheeling to a 27-7 victory over the hapless Cincinnati Bengals yesterday at Paul Brown Stadium. A three-game losing streak, like the touchdown drought, was history.

"It was kind of funny," Dilfer said later, "because it was like we just won the Super Bowl. I had to sit back and say all we did was score a touchdown. I've scored a lot of touchdowns before.

"I was telling myself more than anything ... 'Let's celebrate, let's move on.' "

Said right tackle Harry Swayne: "I never knew there could be so much excitement over scoring a touchdown. It's been so long that I guess it's to be expected."

The final tally on the drought that consumed October: 21 quarters, 60 possessions, 322 minutes and 32 seconds.

"I was just like, 'Yes, the curse is over,' " Ismail said. "The Boston Red Sox are going to the World Series, and they're going to actually win it. That's how I felt."

On the Ravens' bench, the defense offered a silent "Amen."

"Everybody was like, 'Whew, thank you,' " said safety Rod Woodson. "It was really good to see that one go through and our offense get off the skid."

It was actually touchdown times three.

When the Ravens finally found the end zone, they revisited it twice more in the next 12 minutes. Before half-time, Dilfer clicked with tight end Shannon Sharpe on scoring passes of 18 and 19 yards.

Combined with Jamal Lewis' second 100-yard rushing game of the season, two more Matt Stover field goals and another suffocating performance by the defense, the Ravens (6-4) climbed into second place in the AFC Central, ahead of the Pittsburgh Steelers.

Next up are the first-place Tennessee Titans in Nashville. The Titans beat the Steelers, 9-7, yesterday to go 8-1.

"We didn't want to be 5-5 going into Tennessee," said left tackle Jonathan Ogden. "This is a win we needed if we wanted to make the playoffs. I still think we can play better. [But] it's a step in the right direction."

It took the Ravens three possessions and an assist from the defense to find the promised land.

In the waning seconds of the first quarter, penetration by defensive tackle Sam Adams forced a fumbled handoff attempt by Bengals quarterback Akili Smith inside the Cincinnati 20.

Ravens defensive end Michael McCrary recovered at the 16. A third-down penalty against Cincinnati (12 men on the field) gave the Ravens a third-and-eight shot from the 14.

H angle return, a play designed especially for Stokley, restored normalcy to the franchise.

"When Brandon was going to be activated, Brian put that play in for him, because he was killing guys all training camp with that play," said Ismail, who collapsed twice on the field from low blood sugar before returning.

Stokley lined up in the slot to the right side, inside wide receiver Jermaine Lewis. While Lewis ran a post pattern, Stokley ran toward the center of the field, then broke out, behind Lewis. Bengals cornerback Rodney Heath bit on the inside move and never recovered.

Stokley, who was inactive in eight of nine previous games and hadn't played since last season, took the short pass at the 11 and beat Heath to the corner of the end zone.

"It was a good play," said Dilfer, who

It's over

LLOYD FOX

Brandon Stokely eludes Rodney Heath and dives into the corner of the end zone, giving the Ravens their first touchdown in 21 quarters.

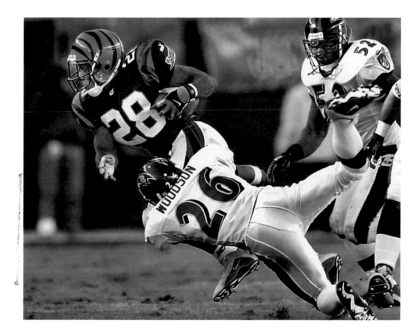

Stuffed again

LLOYD FOX

Corey Dillon, being stopped by Rod Woodson, had another fruitless day against the Ravens, gaining only 23 yards.

Headstand

LLOYD FOX

Rodney Heath's tackle puts the Ravens' Jamal Lewis on his head.

was 23 of 34 for 244 yards. "We knew it had a chance if we got the right coverage. As soon as he went in motion, I knew we had the coverage. It was just a matter of hitting the free throw.

"It was pretty much stealing."

Curiously, Dilfer hit 10 of 13 for 140 yards in the second quarter after his helmet receiver for sideline communication quit. Hand signals and voice instruction sufficed.

Dilfer went to Sharpe three times in the quarter, twice for touchdowns. A seam route opened for an 18-yard score on the heels of a 19-yard reverse by wide receiver Patrick Johnson.

Then, with two minutes left in the half, Dilfer scrambled out of the grasp of defensive end Michael Bankston and threw an improvisational, 19-yard scoring pass to Sharpe.

"When the guy got hold of me, I was fear-stricken," Dilfer said, eliciting laughs. "It was a matter of controlled panic. You try to do something. Sometimes it's ugly, sometimes it's

good. That happened to be good."

Common sense prevailed on a day when Jamal Lewis rumbled for 109 yards and Sharpe had seven catches for 66 yards.

"My thought process going in was, you've got to let the superstars win games when you're in a funk," Dilfer said. "I wanted to get the ball to Shannon and Jamal as much as I could."

The defense did its part. Led by a fourth-quarter, fourth-down run stuff by tackle Tony Siragusa, the Ravens made it another long, futile day for Bengals running back Corey Dillon.

Dillon totaled just 23 yards on 16 carries. In two games and 28 carries against the Ravens this season, he has been tackled behind the line of scrimmage 10 times.

"[The defense] took Corey Dillon away and said if you're going to beat us, you'll have to beat us with Akili throwing the football," Sharpe said. "Today, it didn't happen."

Scoring more

KARL MERTON FERRON

With the touchdown drought over, the Ravens add a score with
a catch by Shannon Sharpe in front of safety Darryl Williams.

Twist and run

KARL MERTON FERRON

Jamal Lewis spins through the
Bengals defense on his way to
another 100-yard game.

Ripped pocket

KARL MERTON FERRON

The Bengals couldn't protect quarterback Akili Smith from James Trapp (38) and Michael McCrary, who combined for a fourth-quarter sack.

We did it, boss

KARL MERTON FERRON

Trent Dilfer celebrates his drought-ending touchdown pass with Ravens president David Modell.

On the road, a Titan-ic victory

By Ken Murray

NASHVILLE, Tenn. — The Ravens beat the Tennessee Titans as much on memory as they did on willpower yesterday.

It was a game of deja vu for tight end Shannon Sharpe, redemption for wide receiver Patrick Johnson and sheer joy for quarterback Trent Dilfer, all of whom had been down this road before.

This time, a nine-play, 70-yard touchdown drive in the last two minutes delivered a dramatic 24-23 victory for the Ravens in the bubbling caldron that was Adelphia Coliseum.

Trailing 23-17 after a Dilfer interception was returned for a touchdown by Perry Phenix, the Ravens had the ball on their own 30 with 2:18 on the clock.

Reminiscent, Sharpe thought, of his career in Denver, where he helped Broncos quarterback John Elway become the NFL's comeback king.

"I told the defense: 'When I come back, I'm coming back with seven points,' " he said later. "A situation like that, they don't believe you. [But] I've been in situations like this so many times with John."

Nine plays later, Johnson made amends for dropping an almost-certain long touchdown pass by catching a game-winning 2-yard throw from Dilfer with 25 seconds left.

It was left for kicker Matt Stover to add the biggest extra point of his season — after Tennessee's Al Del Greco missed his and a subsequent 43-yard field-goal try at the gun. The Ravens' drive may prove to be the biggest of the season, for what it accomplished and what it meant.

"Shannon was so calm in the huddle," said Johnson, the Ravens' third-year wide receiver. "It was amazing to see how calm he was. Trent was poised and calm. They really led us down the field."

The victory boosted the Ravens to 7-4 and within 1½ games of the first-place Titans (8-2) in the AFC Central. It was Tennessee's first-ever loss at Adelphia after 12 straight wins. But more importantly, it stamped Baltimore as a viable playoff team in the AFC.

The Ravens will play four of their last five games at PSINet Stadium, a reward for their arduous early-season road schedule.

At the least, the Ravens are armed with newfound confidence for the stretch run.

"This is a tad bigger than [September's comeback victory over] Jacksonville just because of the situation we're in," said defensive end Michael McCrary. "This is no longer the old Ravens, where we'd lose a game like that at the end. For our offense to be able to keep its poise and patience twice this year is absolutely amazing."

Dilfer was a big part of the poise equation. The seven-year veteran hit 23 of 36 passes for 281 yards, including a perfectly timed, 46-yard touchdown strike to Qadry Ismail in the first quarter.

"Poise has a lot of different faces," Dilfer said. "For some, it's that bland stare and undying confidence. For others, it's an absolute will.

"For me, poise is just trusting the people around me. I've lacked poise in my career because I didn't trust what's going on around me. I told these guys I've worked my whole career to play with a bunch of guys like this."

Dilfer had a sense of deja vu, too. With the score tied at 17 in the fourth quarter, linebacker Peter Boulware had stripped Titans quarterback Steve McNair of the ball. Defensive end Rob Burnett recovered at the Tennessee 22.

But on third down from the 19, with the Ravens positioning for a Stover field goal, Dilfer threw an interception that was returned 87 yards by Phenix for a go-ahead touchdown. The intended receiver was Johnson.

"I've done that four times in my career," Dilfer said, shaking his head. "I've been picked four times on that exact same play, once against Arizona in an identical situation.

"I thought I got 35 [Phenix] to move just enough to get the slant in behind him. You do stupid things once in a while. That was a terrible time to do it."

When Del Greco inexplicably missed the extra point, the six-point deficit hung on the scoreboard as enticement to the Ravens.

"I couldn't believe something that

Embracing victory

Doug Kapustin

Patrick Johnson leaps into the arms of coach Brian Billick after scoring the winning touchdown with 25 seconds left.

Juggling act

Doug Kapustin

Shannon Sharpe bobbles the ball, but holds on for a reception in the first quarter.

good happened to me," Dilfer said.

He regrouped on the bench with a prayer, and then answered one for the Ravens. The pass that got the Ravens into Titans' territory was an ad-lib scramble that became a 36-yard pass to Sharpe.

Flushed out of the pocket to his right on third-and-five, Dilfer found Sharpe on a sideline adjustment to the Tennessee 29.

"Shannon's sense of timing when a quarterback is out of the pocket is like nothing I've seen in my life," Dilfer said. "It's like we're reading each other's minds."

Although Sharpe made the catch and rolled out of bounds on the play, officials at first ruled him down inbounds. Because he had not been touched before going out, the ruling was corrected and the Ravens regained not only five seconds on the clock, but their second timeout as well.

From there, there was a 3-yard toss to Jermaine Lewis out of the backfield, a 5-yard pass to Sharpe and an incompletion in the end zone. On fourth-and-two from the 21, Dilfer lobbed a fade pass for Ismail at the goal line. The ball fell incomplete when Dainon Sidney ran into Ismail, and the ensuing pass interference call gave the Ravens first-and-goal at the 2.

After a no-gain run by Jamal Lewis (99 yards on 23 carries), Dilfer stopped the clock at 29 seconds with a spike. Then Ravens coach Brian Billick called a "Change Left Zeke, Quick Sprint Right 17," with Johnson as the primary receiver.

It was double redemption for Johnson, who not only dropped a would-be touchdown throw earlier in the game, but also dropped another one in the end zone a year ago here in a 14-11 loss to the Titans.

"It was the exact same scenario as last year," Johnson said. "I had to face my demons from last year, too. I can't believe I had the opportunity to make another play."

Johnson lined up in the slot to the right, inside Ismail. While Ismail drove to the corner of the end zone, taking cornerback Denard Walker with him, Johnson raced toward the sideline with Samari Rolle in pursuit.

Rolle tangled momentarily with Johnson, who made the catch and managed to get both feet down in bounds in the end zone.

The Ravens still had to survive one last challenge from the Titans. A kickoff return to the Tennessee 44, an 11-yard pass and a 20-yard scramble by McNair set up Del Greco for a 43-yard field-goal attempt to win the game. Del Greco was wide right, turning Tennessee's cheers into tears.

Right tackle Harry Swayne isn't sure the Ravens have seen the last of the Titans — or Adelphia — this season.

"I wouldn't be surprised if we have to come back here for the playoffs," Swayne said. "If that's the case, it'd be like we've been here, let's do it again."

Door closed

DOUG KAPUSTIN

Eddie George finds his way blocked by a Ravens defensive swarm.

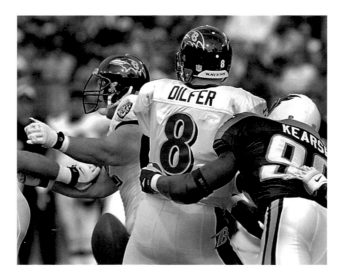

Knocked loose

DOUG KAPUSTIN

The Titans' Jevon Kearse strips the ball from Trent Dilfer, but the Ravens recover.

Wide shot

KARL MERTON FERRON

Al Del Greco (3) tries what would have been a game-winning field goal as Cornell Brown leaps in an attempt to block it. The kick went wide right.

Take it away

KARL MERTON FERRON

Peter Boulware knocks the ball from Steve McNair for a turnover during the fourth quarter.

Celebrate good times

Doug Kapustin

Brian Billick reacts to the go-ahead touch-down in the fourth quarter.

GAME 12: Ravens 27, Cowboys 0
November 19, 2000 • PSINet Stadium, Baltimore

Defense adds a zero to impressive total

By Ken Murray

The most defiant defense in the NFL can't say the P-word, but it can use the S-word. And the Ravens speak the language of shutouts eloquently.

Ravaging a once-proud Dallas Cowboys' offense, 27-0, before 69,416 at PSINet Stadium, the Ravens' defense yesterday climbed another rung on a ladder only a few have dared to scale.

Their fourth shutout of the regular season is the second-most in the NFL's Super Bowl era, one behind the 1976 Pittsburgh Steelers.

Their eighth win of the season — tying the franchise high — leaves them positioned well for the stretch run to the postseason. Indeed, if the playoffs started today, the 8-4 Ravens would claim the AFC's top wild-card seed and Baltimore's first home playoff game since 1977.

"For us to win in the dominating fashion we did says something about us," said coach Brian Billick, who last week banned all discussion within Ravens ranks about the playoffs. "This is a special group, and they have earned the right to talk about [shutouts]."

The domination was so complete, the game was never in doubt once the Ravens opened a 17-0 first-half lead.

It was so thorough that rookie running back Jamal Lewis had his third 100-yard game of the season with four minutes left in the first half.

It was so convincing on national TV that few teams will relish a postseason matchup against this defense.

"It was a great statement to blank the Cowboys like we did," said linebacker Jamie Sharper. "It shows we're ready for all comers, that we can beat anybody on a given day, that we can dominate any team."

The offense rolled up a franchise-record 250 rushing yards — 187 by Lewis in a powerful performance — and the defense allowed Dallas to cross midfield just three times. The Cowboys (4-7) never got any closer to the goal line than the Baltimore 28-yard line. That third-quarter opportunity dissolved, however, when rookie kicker Tim Seder was wide right and short on a 46-yard field-goal attempt.

Outgained 479-192 in total yards, the Cowboys suffered their first shutout since Sept. 15, 1991, a 24-0 loss to the Philadelphia Eagles.

"They're an awfully good group," Cowboys quarterback Troy Aikman said, "but I don't think that anybody is so good in this league that you shouldn't be able to go down and score some points. So that's a reflection on the way we played as well."

The Ravens are good enough to contemplate breaking the Steelers' post-merger record of five shutouts. If they can't talk about the playoffs, they are more than willing to give a discourse on defense.

"Now it's in reach," said middle linebacker Ray Lewis on the possibility of six shutouts. "Now we go for it. We can taste it, smell it. So why not go for it?"

"That's a goal every week, a realistic goal every week," said linebacker Peter Boulware. "We'll definitely shoot for it [the record]. But our first thing is the win."

The Ravens pounded the Cowboys at the line of scrimmage. First they took away the run, then they took away hope.

"The key today was to play physical gap control, and play hard," said defensive tackle Sam Adams. "Play until you're tired and exhausted, until you have to drop."

It's a defense that prides itself on going the extra mile.

"We have two things you can't coach," said defensive end Rob Burnett. "Attitude and effort. Our guys have an attitude and they give 100 percent. We answered the call today. That was the best offensive line we've faced this year."

Although defensive end Michael McCrary got the Ravens' only sack, they harassed Aikman into three interceptions. Safety Rod Woodson got his 58th career theft in the second quarter and it led to a touchdown. Safety Corey Harris got another second-quarter pick, and Lewis had a fourth-quarter interception on a pass tipped by Burnett.

For the third straight week, the offense made it a collaborative effort. Jamal Lewis delivered the second-best rushing performance in franchise history (Priest Holmes rushed for 227 yards at Cincinnati in 1998), and quar-

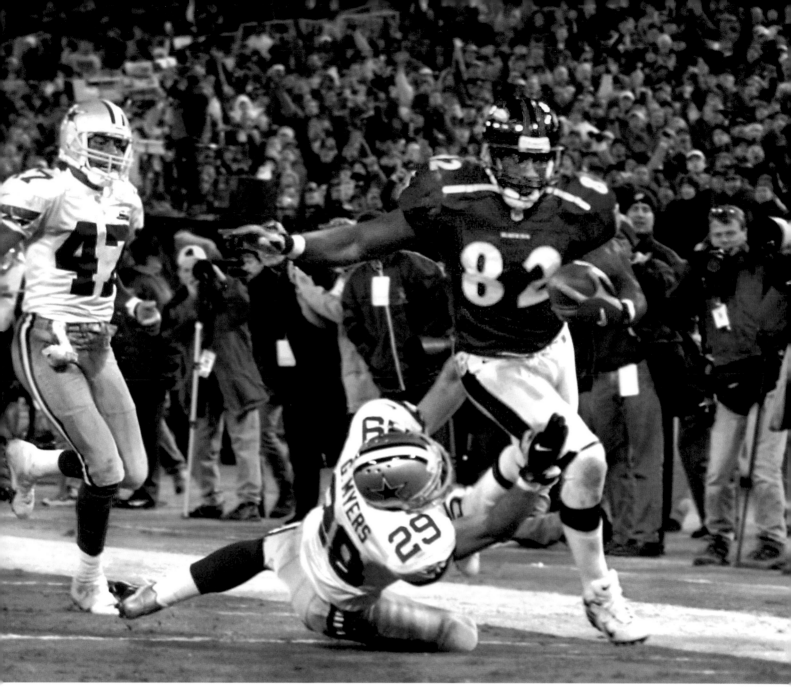

No stopping him

John Makely

Shannon Sharpe leaves Cowboys in his wake on the way to a touchdown.

Shutdown

Kenneth K. Lam

Emmitt Smith discovers what other running backs already have learned: It's hard to run against the Ravens.

Behind the defense

John Makely

Shannon Sharpe, being pursued by Dexter Coakley (52) and Dat Nguyen, heads for the end zone.

Good hands man

Kenneth K. Lam

Brandon Stokley (below) makes a diving catch at the 4, setting up a field goal for the Ravens.

Fall of Troy

John Makely

Peter Boulware grabs Troy
Aikman as he tries to pass in
the fourth quarter.

terback Trent Dilfer completed 18 of 24
passes for 242 yards and two touchdowns.

Dilfer's 40-yard touchdown strike to
split end Qadry Ismail was the Ravens'
first touchdown on their opening possession this season. His 59-yard scoring
pass to tight end Shannon Sharpe in the
second quarter — after Woodson's interception — gave the defense more than
enough room to work.

Interestingly, Dilfer has played with
two of the league's top defenses of this
era. Last season, he played with the
Tampa Bay Buccaneers.

"This defense is playing better, but it's
very similar in that they're both relent-
less," he said. "They'll hit you until you
want to give up. This defense is more
big-play oriented. "I have a great deal of
respect for the defense in Tampa Bay.
Those guys saved my butt a million
times, and I appreciate them deeply.
[But] with four shutouts, you've got to
give the edge to Baltimore."

Tough day

Lloyd Fox

Troy Aikman
watches a replay
of a Ravens
touchdown on
the PSINet
Stadium video
board.

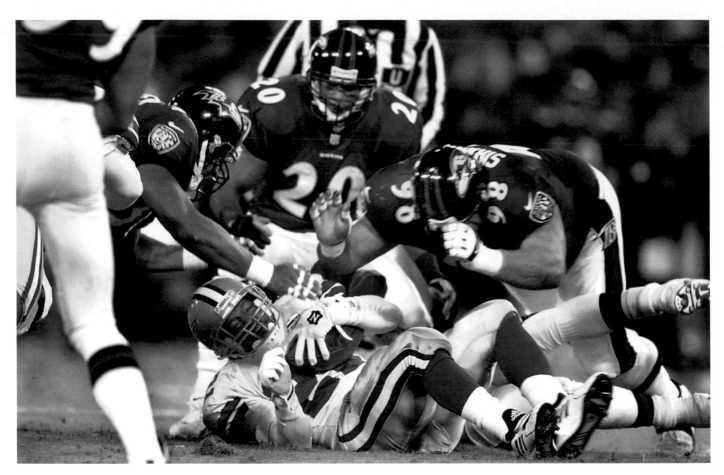

Ganging up

KENNETH K. LAM

Ravens surround
Emmitt Smith, making
sure he's down.

His name
is Chad?

LLOYD FOX

A fan finds
more certainty
in his allegiance
to the Ravens
than in the
presidential
election.

Happy QB

LLOYD FOX

Trent Dilfer leaps into a lineman's arms after throwing a touchdown pass to Qadry Ismail.

GAME 13: Ravens 44, Browns 7
November 26, 2000 • PSINet Stadium, Baltimore

Jamal Lewis takes the ball and runs with it

By Ken Murray

After 13 weeks, a change of quarterbacks and the arrival of a phenom running back, the Ravens' true offensive personality has finally emerged.

This may be Brian Billick's passing offense, but it is suddenly Jamal Lewis' ball. And he's not giving it up.

Climbing on Lewis' broad back, the Ravens crushed the Cleveland Browns for a landmark 44-7 win yesterday before 68,361 at PSINet Stadium. The Ravens' ninth victory against four losses assured the franchise of its first winning season, but it was a game that said more about where the team was headed than where it has been.

Counting Tennessee's 16-13 loss to Jacksonville, the Ravens coast into their bye week just a half-game behind the Titans (9-3) in the AFC Central. Should Tennessee lose in Philadelphia next week — a distinct possibility — the Ravens, with four straight wins, would be tied for the division lead and in control of their own playoff destiny.

Lewis gouged the Browns for 170 yards and two touchdowns on a season-high 30 carries to create his own imprint. The Ravens also got two touchdown passes from quarterback Trent Dilfer, 461 yards in total offense and still another stifling defensive effort in ringing up the biggest winning margin of their five-year history. This is a profile of a team that could turn heads — and level bodies — in January.

"This is something substantial for us," said Billick, the wonder-worker of the Ravens' two-year turnaround. "It classifies us in a certain way. We can take a lot of satisfaction in 1½ years having built to this point."

Lewis, the fifth pick in this year's draft, broke Priest Holmes' single-season rushing record of 1,008 yards yesterday, cruising to 1,095 in just 10 starts. With 357 rushing yards in the past two weeks, he gives the Ravens an identity they've never before enjoyed.

"If I were to characterize it, I would say we are a running team that has the ability to strike deep if you commit too many people to the run," said left tackle Jonathan Ogden. "Those are the best teams, in my opinion, that can run the ball at will, but also have the ability to go vertical. That's what Atlanta was a couple years ago when they went to the Super Bowl."

The injury-depleted Browns (3-10) stunned the Ravens with a four-play, 86-yard touchdown drive on their first series. Operating out of a no-huddle, empty-backfield mode, the Browns got a 67-yard pass from Doug Pederson to Kevin Johnson — the longest play against the Ravens this season — and a 4-yard touchdown run from Travis Prentice for a 7-0 lead.

"If it was execution, then we'd have been scared," middle linebacker Ray Lewis said of the first first-drive touchdown they've surrendered this season. "But we just missed tackles."

The Ravens weren't scared. The Browns gained just 3 net yards the rest of the half and didn't get another first down until the final 1:50 of the second quarter. They finished with just five first downs, a new defensive low for the Ravens.

The offense responded with 44 unanswered points, most in franchise history. Dilfer supplied the vertical game with a 46-yard touchdown pass to flanker Patrick Johnson, who made a spectacular adjustment on the ball at the 2-yard line. Dilfer, completing 12 of 23 for 169 yards, also threw a 2-yard scoring pass to fullback Sam Gash in a 24-point second-quarter binge.

But the real ramrod of this victory was the precocious Jamal Lewis. He went over middle linebacker Wali Rainer for a 1-yard touchdown run in the first quarter, and bolted 36 yards in the second to open a 31-7 lead.

Nobody appreciates Lewis more than Billick. When asked about the wall that rookies usually run into late in the season, the coach gave his unqualified endorsement: "Well, he's running over it, through it, around it and anywhere it shows up."

Lewis has rushed for 565 yards in his past four games, 658 in his past five. His presence is such that the Ravens have run 95 times in the past two games, compared with 51 passes (including sacks).

"I love when we stick with the running game, because it shows our dominance over the other team," said left guard Edwin Mulitalo.

Clearing a hurdle

LLOYD FOX

Jamal Lewis leaps
through the Browns to
the Ravens' first touch-
down. Lewis broke the
team record for season
rushing yards in the
game.

Knockout

LLOYD FOX

Corey Harris (45) jars the ball loose from Browns punt returner Dennis Northcutt.

No one expects more from Lewis than Lewis himself.

"I'm not trying to be just any running back," he said. "I'm trying to be great. I want to be great. Whatever is going to make me great, that's what I'm trying to do."

He is already special in Dilfer's eyes.

"He can beat you with speed, he can run you over," Dilfer said. "He's developing a presence in the passing game. He's a very good blocker.

"When he becomes as good a blocker and receiver as he is a runner, he's going to be the best in the league."

Ravens tight end Shannon Sharpe concurred, but threw out one important qualifier.

"I see a lot of guys come in the first year and have success, and then they don't do the things it took to get to that position," Sharpe said. "He'll have to work harder, because the level of expectation he sets for himself and what people set for him is going to be higher."

The Ravens closed out their AFC Central schedule with an 8-2 record. That record, and their AFC mark of 8-3, could prove critical in a potential tiebreaker scenario with the Titans, with whom they split.

At the very least, the Ravens are poised for a strong finishing run. They averaged 470 total yards the past two weeks. In the past three, Dilfer has thrown four touchdown passes of longer than 40 yards. It is an offense preparing to make a playoff statement.

"It says when we execute, we can do whatever we want to do," Johnson said. "It has nothing to do with the defense out there. If we execute our plays, it doesn't matter who is out there."

All that matters at this point is who is in the way.

Rare glory

Doug Kapustin

Fullback Sam Gash, normally just a blocker, celebrates his touchdown catch.

Our ball

Doug Kapustin

Rob Burnett comes up with the ball on a Browns fumble.

Loose Goose

Doug Kapustin

Tony Siragusa gets by blocker
Everett Linsday to pressure quarterback Spergon Wynn.

Coach's signal

LLOYD FOX

Brian Billick knows where Jamal Lewis is headed – for a 36-yard touchdown.

Twinkle-toes

LLOYD FOX

Priest Holmes dances into the end zone in the fourth quarter.

GAME 14: Ravens 24, Chargers 3

December 14, 2000 • PSINet Stadium, Baltimore

Celebrating
a berth day

BY KEN MURRAY

This is why Shannon Sharpe came to Baltimore after 10 years in Denver.

It's why Rob Burnett came back for his 11th NFL season.

It's why Brian Billick came from Minnesota a year ago.

Playoff football became a reality for the Ravens yesterday when they rumbled past the San Diego Chargers, 24-3, in the cold and rain of a December homestretch at PSINet Stadium. Their fifth straight victory secured the first postseason berth of their Baltimore tenure, and made a lot of career decisions look inspired in hindsight.

"The reason I didn't retire, the reason I came back here, is because of this," said Burnett, who began his career with the Cleveland Browns and figures to finish it here with the Ravens. "I thought [making a playoff run] was a strong possibility. I felt like I'd be missing out, that I'd be cheated, if I didn't come back because I helped build this thing."

Burnett, 33, helped nail down the playoff spot yesterday with a tap-dance fumble recovery that belied his size (6 feet 4, 270 pounds) and position (defensive end). The Ravens were protecting a 10-3 lead in the third quarter when Chargers running back Terrell Fletcher scampered around right end from inside his own 15. He had one man to beat for a big play, when safety Kim Herring not only made the tackle, but dislodged the ball as well with a helmet hit to the chest. When it caromed back toward the goal line, Burnett made a nimble sideline move to retrieve and recover the ball at the 3-yard line.

Two plays later, running back Jamal Lewis made another athletic play, hurdling defensive end Al Fontenot for a 1-yard touchdown run and 17-3 lead. Everything that followed was academic.

The turnover was one of five on the day for the Ravens (10-4), who cashed in 21 points in the exchange. It was significant on a day when the Ravens' offense showed the rust of a bye week and the effects of a steady rain.

Burnett's athleticism did not go unnoticed by his teammates.

"I'm going to call him Fred Astaire," Herring said. "Anybody else would have dove on it, but he picked it up."

The Ravens took turns making Chargers quarterback Ryan Leaf look like a first-round bust. There was linebacker Cornell Brown's magnificent sack-and-strip that preceded a 28-yard touchdown pass from Trent Dilfer to Qadry Ismail in the second quarter. There was cornerback Chris McAlister's second-quarter interception when Leaf (9-for-23 for 78 yards) overthrew intended receiver Curtis Conway by 10 yards. There was linebacker Jamie Sharper's first-quarter fumble recovery after Leaf mishandled the center snap from Roman Fortin.

Leaf had no culpability, however, in the fifth turnover. That was purely the work of James Trapp, who alertly knocked blocker DeRon Jenkins into punt returner Nate Jacquet, sending both to the ground on a 27-yard punt by Kyle Richardson to the 13. The ball hit the prone Jenkins — a former Raven — and was recovered by Brad Jackson. That was the 39th takeaway of the season for the Ravens.

On third-and-15, Dilfer (16-for-24 for 187 yards, two touchdowns and two interceptions) found wide receiver Brandon Stokley for a 22-yard touchdown. Game, set, match.

The win boosted the Ravens' conference record to 9-3, second to Miami's 8-2 in the AFC. They may be a wild-card entry, but in Billick's second year as coach, the Ravens aren't shy about their Super Bowl aspirations.

"Brian told us greed is good," said Herring. "The playoffs are great, but we want it all."

Billick laid down his playoff goal as soon as last year's 8-8 season was finished.

"At the end of the year, we stood up and said anything less than the playoffs would be unsuccessful, not only for this year but last year," he said. "So to stand up and be accountable that way, and to live up to what you said you were going to do, sometimes is undervalued, and my hat's off to those guys in the [locker] room."

Freedom of speech returned to that locker room yesterday, too, when Billick finally lifted his ban of the word "playoffs."

"One word, two syllables," said

Handy man

LLOYD FOX

Qadry Ismail hauls in a second-quarter touchdown pass that the Chargers' Fakhir Brown can't reach.

His day

KARL MERTON FERRON

Owner Art Modell, introduced on the field before the game, waves to the PSINet Stadium crowd.

Diver

KARL MERTON
FERRON

Trent Dilfer
lays out for
extra yards in
the first
quarter.

Sharpe, the free-agent tight end who joined the team in February. "Playoff. It feels real good.

"I said at the beginning of the year, one of the main reasons I came here was to play in January. We still have two games to go, Arizona and the [New York] Jets. We're jockeying for position.

"The goal was to get in the playoffs. Now it's a crapshoot. We've got just as good a chance as anyone else to get to Tampa [site of Super Bowl XXXV]."

Super Bowl-bound?

"We're definitely capable of getting there," McAlister said. "If we continue to dominate, we'll have a full head of steam going into the playoffs."

This will be Burnett's first trip to the postseason since he played with the 1994 Browns, who beat New England before losing at Pittsburgh.

He doesn't want a short visit.

"We're not going to the playoffs just to play one game," he said. "We're in the playoffs, but right now we have to keep the hammer down and stay focused. We're having much more fun with this team than I did [in 1994]."

January football was the lure that got Burnett back this season. It was also the hook that helped bring in defensive tackle Tony Siragusa — invaluable in the team's top-ranked run defense — from an acrimonious training-camp holdout last summer.

"I called him every day, saying, 'You don't want to miss this,' " Burnett said. "Our days in the league are numbered. We might as well go for the golden goose all we can."

In Baltimore, playoff football is back.

Too late

LLOYD FOX

DeRon Jenkins, a former Raven, tackles Brandon Stokley, but he's already scored a touchdown.

Crumbled Leaf

LLOYD FOX

Ray Lewis (52) and Rob Burnett sack Ryan Leaf, forcing a fumble.

Paying
the price

KARL MERTON
FERRON

The Chargers'
Curtis Conway
makes a catch
and recovers his
fumble, but is
sandwiched by
Jamie Sharper
(55) and Ray
Lewis.

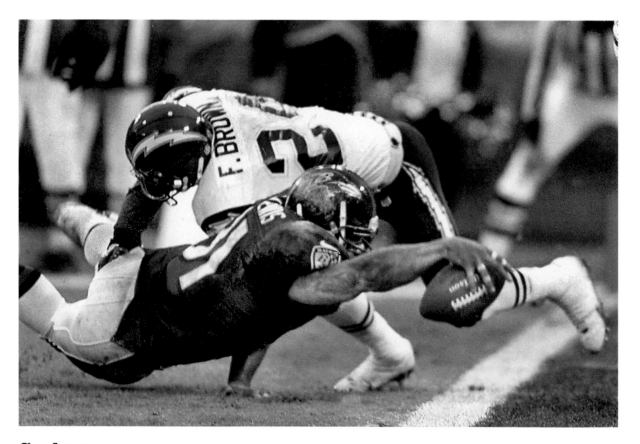

So close

LLOYD FOX

Jamal Lewis tries to
stretch for a touch-
down while being
tackled by Fakhir
Brown. The Ravens
scored on the next
play.

We're in

John Makely

Trent Dilfer acknowledges the fans in celebrating the Ravens' playoff berth.

GAME 15: Ravens 13, Cardinals 7

December 17, 2000 • Sun Devil Stadium, Tempe, Ariz.

After wandering in desert, Ravens find their way

By Ken Murray

TEMPE, Ariz. — On a weekend when AFC playoff teams were riddled by upsets, the Ravens proved bulletproof in a desert ambush.

They survived a questionable replay reversal yesterday, got two huge turnovers by linebacker Jamie Sharper and just enough offense to squeeze past the gritty Arizona Cardinals, 13-7, before a sparse crowd of 37,452 at Sun Devil Stadium.

When the smoke of Week 16 cleared, the Ravens (11-4) had assured themselves of no worse than a home game in the wild-card round. Beyond that, the scenario gets murky. But if the Ravens beat the New York Jets next week at home, and the Tennessee Titans lose to the Dallas Cowboys the following Monday night, they would gain the No. 1 seed in the AFC playoffs by virtue of tiebreakers over both the Titans and the Oakland Raiders.

Suddenly, the Ravens have the NFL's longest winning streak (six games), thanks to Denver's 20-7 loss at Kansas City yesterday. Clinching the first home playoff game for a Baltimore team since 1977 was the reward.

"It's big," said quarterback Trent Dilfer. "You see what can happen when you go on the road. At home, you can get your guns blazing.

"That doesn't mean we can't win on the road. We've done it. But I'd be lying if I said we didn't prefer to play at home."

The Ravens were living dangerously in Arizona. The 3-12 Cardinals finished with more first downs (18-14) and more total yards (309-214) than Baltimore, and had three possessions in the red zone. When quarterback Jake Plummer (23-for-43 for 266 yards) teamed with wide receiver Frank Sanders for a 27-yard touchdown five minutes into the second half, the Ravens trailed (7-3) for the first time in 21 quarters. The touchdown came when safety Rod Woodson went for an interception and cornerback Chris McAlister missed a diving leg tackle as Sanders pulled into the open field.

The Ravens answered in a style that has become commonplace — with huge plays on defense. There were two sacks by defensive end Rob Burnett, a spectacular stuff on a fourth-and-one quarterback sneak by defensive tackle Sam Adams and, for a finishing touch, a dramatic fourth-down knockdown of Plummer's pass by middle linebacker Ray Lewis, who also had 13 tackles.

Turnovers were the theme in this win, though.

Two minutes after Arizona's touchdown, Sharper delivered the first of his two game-changing plays. After the Ravens' offense had gone three-plays-and-out, Sharper intercepted Plummer's second pass, literally pulling it out of tight end Chris Gedney's hands. He lumbered 45 yards down the field to the Arizona 6, picking up a key block from McAlister along the way.

"I read his route and broke on it," Sharper said.

On third-and-goal, running back Jamal Lewis hurdled into the end zone for a 1-yard touchdown, following center Jeff Mitchell and fullback Sam Gash for a 10-7 lead. That run and a pair of 42-yard field goals by Matt Stover accounted for all of Baltimore's scoring.

Lewis finished with 126 rushing yards to become the 14th rookie to gain 1,300 rushing yards. He also had a fourth-quarter fumble on a swing pass that looked crucial until Sharper forced his fifth fumble of the season one play later. Lewis' fumble gave Arizona possession on the Ravens' 15 with 12:20 left in the game. Disaster loomed when tight end Terry Hardy caught a short pass from Plummer and bolted toward the end zone. At the 5, Sharper caught him from behind and deftly knocked the ball out with a right-hand swipe. Woodson recovered in a mad scramble at the 5.

"He didn't see me coming from the back side," Sharper said. "That's something we work on in practice every day."

The defense came up with four turnovers on the day. Woodson's punishing hit on Michael Pittman at the Baltimore 7 in the first quarter knocked the ball loose and the Arizona running back out of the game with a concussion. The fumble was recovered by Lewis. Cornerback

Parting red sea

KENNETH K. LAM

Behind blocks by Jeff Mitchell (left) and Harry Swayne (70), Jamal Lewis jumps through a hole for a touchdown.

Cornering ability

KENNETH K. LAM

Duane Starks runs back an
interception, avoiding a tackle attempt by Thomas Jones.

Duane Starks owned the other turnover, returning a second-quarter interception 30 yards.

The Cardinals had one last chance to win, however. They got the ball at their own 40 with 7:46 left. Rookie running back Thomas Jones (39 rushing yards, 41 receiving yards) got the ball on seven of nine plays as they drove to the 12-yard line. A false start penalty pushed the Cardinals back to the 17.

Then, with 2:32 left and Plummer in the pocket, linebacker Peter Boulware knocked the ball loose on an apparent fumble that was recovered by Woodson. But the Cardinals issued a replay challenge, and won when it was ruled that Plummer had attempted a shovel pass.

"I thought it was bad," Boulware said of the call. "[The official] said the quarterback had his arm going forward, but I think I knocked it out."

Woodson concurred, but added the caveat.

"You have to live with rough calls," he said. "You have to overcome it. We had

to make two more plays on defense, and we did that."

On third-and-10 from the Baltimore 17, safety Corey Harris stopped Jones for a 5-yard gain on a dump pass over the middle. On fourth down, Lewis rejected a quick slant pass from Plummer and danced off the field.

"I just made a play," Lewis said. "He has been throwing the ball quick all game, and I just played off him."

Said Adams: "Things were hairy, but we buckled down and came out with a win. It's not always as pretty as you'd like."

Especially on offense, where Dilfer threw for just 70 yards and had one critical interception in the end zone after Starks' interception gave the Ravens a first down at the Cardinals' 5.

"You don't fear an opponent, [but] you respect them," said tight end Shannon Sharpe, open in the end zone on the interception. "I don't think we showed them the respect they should have gotten."

Tangle of arms

DOUG KAPUSTIN

Duane Starks reaches up to break up a pass intended for David Boston, but is called for interference.

Not in
the Cards

Kenneth K. Lam

Arizona's Rob
Frederickson
brings down
Trent Dilfer for a
loss in the fourth
quarter.

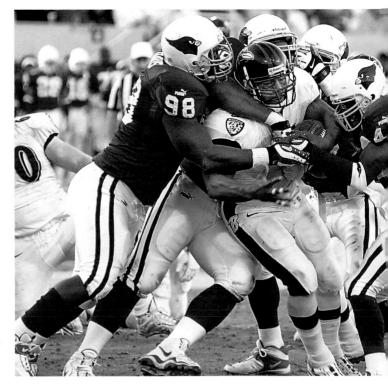

Tough
to tackle

Kenneth K. Lam

A common sight
during the 2000
season: Jamal
Lewis dragging
along a group of
defenders before
being stopped.

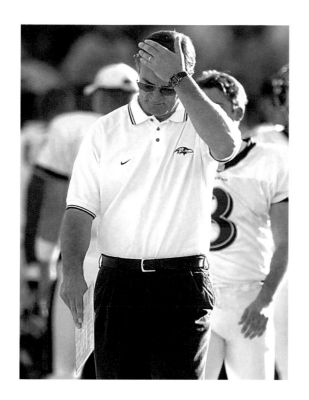

Feeling heat

DOUG KAPUSTIN

Brian Billick couldn't relax during his team's tight victory over the Cardinals.

Not a good day

DOUG KAPUSTIN

The Ravens struggled on offense at Arizona, as on this dropped pass by tight end Shannon Sharpe.

GAME 16: Ravens 34, Jets 20

December 24, 2000 • PSINet Stadium, Baltimore

Defense gets the last word

By Ken Murray

The Ravens' record-setting defense sat in a downtown hotel Saturday night and seethed as New York Jets coach Al Groh delivered a mocking taunt on videotape. In so many calculated words from a news conference on Wednesday, Groh sarcastically suggested the Jets had no chance against Baltimore's dominating defense.

Yesterday, the Ravens answered with one of their most frenetic efforts of a record-setting season. The rebuttal featured six suffocating turnovers, three goal-line stands and a wild, 34-20 victory at PSINet Stadium before 69,184 that eliminated the Jets from postseason play.

In the end, Baltimore survived a vintage passing performance by ex-Ravens quarterback Vinny Testaverde — 69 pass attempts, 481 yards, three interceptions — to advance to the playoffs with a seven-game winning streak. If Tennessee beats Dallas tonight as expected, the Ravens will enter as the fourth seed in the AFC and draw a wild-card home game at 12:30 p.m. Sunday against the Denver Broncos.

The 12-4 Ravens wasted little time yesterday regurgitating Groh's ill-conceived remarks about their defense.

"Tell Al Groh his third-grade reverse psychology didn't work," defensive end Rob Burnett said. "Not to disrespect the Jets players, but Al Groh was the one who fueled the fire this week. He didn't believe, but he believes now."

Added defensive tackle Tony Siragusa: "I also want to thank Al Groh. He said we were the best defense in football, and that gave us a lot of confidence going into the game."

The Ravens walked away with NFL records for fewest points (165) and rushing yards (970) allowed in a 16-game season. They tied a team record with six turnovers, including a 98-yard interception return for a touchdown by cornerback Chris McAlister.

They needed every one of them on a day when Testaverde nearly matched Drew Bledsoe's single-game NFL record of 70 pass attempts (1994). His 481 yards represented the most ever by a Ravens opponent. As fate would have it, Testaverde owns the Ravens record for passing yards in a game with 429, set in 1996. Testaverde accounted for five of those turnovers himself.

"If you throw 69 times, I expect you to put up some yards," said McAlister, whose touchdown return just before the half gave the Ravens their first — and final — lead of the day at 20-14. "I also expect our defense to respond the way we did. Our defense is capable of getting four or five interceptions."

The Ravens got three yesterday — cornerback Duane Starks got the other two — to thwart the Jets. Three times the Jets had the ball inside the Ravens' 10, but the only points they got came on a 19-yard field goal by Brett Conway in the fourth quarter. The game was a statistical nightmare for the Ravens. They were outgained, 524-142, in total offense. They produced only five first downs — a team record low — against 22 for New York. They ran only 55 plays to the Jets' 91.

For the second straight week, the Ravens' offense sputtered. Turnovers led to 20 second-quarter points that wiped out a 14-0 deficit. In the second half, punt returner Jermaine Lewis dazzled with touchdown runs of 54 and 89 yards to keep the Jets at a comfortable distance.

The frustration was visible for quarterback Trent Dilfer, who completed just 11 of 25 passes for 99 yards, one touchdown and two interceptions. In his past two games, Dilfer is 23 for 47 for 169 yards, one touchdown and three interceptions.

"We really felt we were going to play good this week," he said. "We knew it'd be ugly. [But] we felt at the end of 60 minutes, we were going to make enough plays to feel good about it.

"That's what's most discouraging. We did not make any plays except for the touchdown."

Except for a 7-yard touchdown pass to split end Qadry Ismail in the second quarter — five plays after Keith Washington recovered a fumbled center snap at the New York 42-— Dilfer did not complete a pass to a wide receiver. That was as many passes as he completed to himself; Dilfer caught his own pass in the second quarter after it was batted back by defensive

Safety in numbers

KENNETH K. LAM

Chris McAlister and Ray Lewis know the signal for a safety, and the defense has just recorded one against the Jets.

Specialists

Kenneth K. Lam

Corey Harris, Brad Jackson, Kim Herring and O.J. Brigance (left to right) team up to stop Leon Johnson on a kickoff return.

tackle Jason Ferguson.

"Obviously, we have to get the offense cranked up better than we've shown the last two weeks, or it's going to be a struggle," coach Brian Billick said. "But the way these guys take care of each other, we'll take wins any way you can.

"To win 34-20 playing the way we did comprehensively against a team as desperate as they were, that speaks well."

The Jets even held rookie running back Jamal Lewis in check. Lewis finished with 52 yards on 22 carries, an average of 2.4.

"The bottom line is, we need to play better," left tackle Jonathan Ogden said. "We've got to hit harder; everybody has to do better. There's no magic formula for playing football. But we can't afford to get into that lapse we had early in the year."

The Ravens at least avoided a potential disaster when both Dilfer and backup

Tony Banks had to leave the game with injuries. Dilfer suffered a sprained ligament in his left wrist on the Ravens' last possession of the half. Although X-rays were negative, Billick opted to have Banks start the second half. On his third play, he slipped retreating to the pocket, then took a hit on his left shoulder as he made a 2-yard gain. Dilfer returned at that point and finished the game. He said he should not miss any practice time. Banks' X-rays showed a separated shoulder that makes him questionable for the potential wild-card game. He left the locker room with his arm in a sling.

"I should be fine," Banks said, "because it was my non-throwing shoulder."

The Ravens hope they can say the same for their offense.

Tight grip

KENNETH K. LAM

The Jets' Victor Green has no chance to wrest this reception from the hands of Shannon Sharpe.

Thievery

KENNETH K. LAM

Duane Starks intercepts a pass and avoids receiver Dedric Ward. The Ravens intercepted Vinny Testaverde three times.

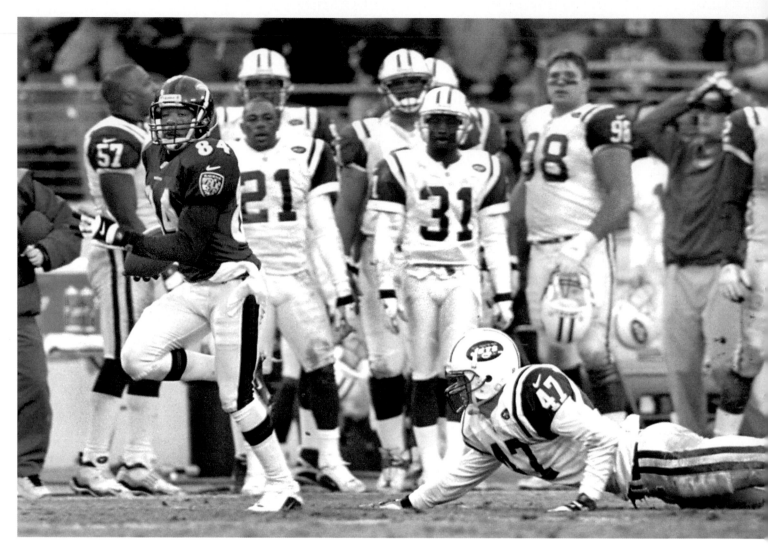

That man again

Kenneth K. Lam

Jermaine Lewis takes off past Scott Frost on his way to a second punt return for a touchdown.

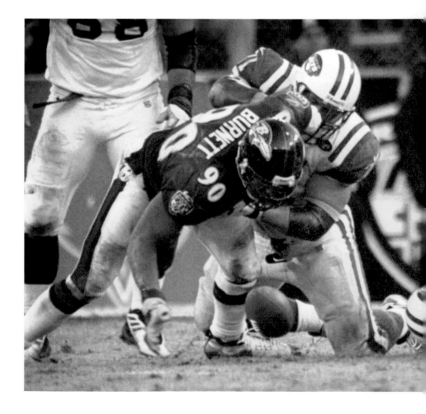

Alert play

Karl Merton Ferron

Rob Burnett shrugs off a Jets offensive lineman to fall on a fumble by Vinny Testaverde.

Big turn-around

Karl Merton Ferron

Chris McAlister takes off on a 98-yard interception return for a touchdown right before halftime.

Another pass

Kenneth K. Lam

Vinny Testaverde prepares to launch one of his 69 passes. He threw for 481 yards in the loss.

Ravens 21, Broncos 3

December 31, 2000 • PSINet Stadium, Baltimore

More evidence
for the defense

By Ken Murray

In a postseason defined by defense, the Ravens struck an ominous pose yesterday. Super Bowl contender.

On the heels of a 21-3 wild-card dismantling of the Denver Broncos, the Ravens suddenly look like a very tough team to beat.

Maybe even the team to beat.

"I think so," said defensive end Michael McCrary, after his three-sack effort underscored another dominating performance. "Defense wins championships. We went down in history this year when we broke two records for defense."

The Ravens (13-4) are trying to make history now by becoming the second straight AFC Central wild-card team to reach the Super Bowl. The road winds through Adelphia Coliseum, where they'll renew a fierce division rivalry with the Tennessee Titans in a playoff game Sunday at 12:30 p.m.

They split the season series with Tennessee, losing at home on Oct. 22, 14-6, and winning in Nashville on Nov. 12, 24-23. The Ravens are the only visiting team to win in Adelphia in the Titans' two seasons there.

"I'm not sure how many people thought we would go back there, given the circumstances," Ravens coach Brian Billick said. "There's a great deal of respect between these two teams, and I think they knew we were going back there, and we knew we were going to be back there. It's going to be a hell of a game."

Yesterday's game — played in wind gusts of up to 27 mph with a wind-chill factor of 5 degrees — brought Baltimore's tenacious defense to a new high. Discredited for playing a soft schedule in a soft division, the Ravens systematically destroyed one of the NFL's best offenses.

A record crowd of 69,638 at PSINet Stadium watched as the Ravens allowed the league's second-ranked offense just 42 rushing yards and 177 total yards. The Broncos crossed midfield only once, got as far as the 12, and settled for a 31-yard field goal by Jason Elam.

Defensive tackle Tony Siragusa made a big stop at the 12 when he hurdled Denver guard Dan Neil to tackle Anderson for no gain on third-and-one.

For Ravens offensive tackle Harry Swayne, who had played two seasons with the Broncos, the shutdown was a revelation.

"I was kind of surprised we were able to do that to them," Swayne said. "I know how Denver prides itself on offense, but they had out-and-out total breakdowns.

"Receivers were dropping balls, and they never drop balls. It's not the weather, either, because it's just as bad out in Denver. I think they were a little surprised by how hard we bring it."

The Ravens brought it hard enough that 1,500-yard rusher Mike Anderson was held to 40 yards on 15 carries. The inability to run, along with a second-quarter deficit, chased the Broncos out of the running game in the second half.

The key issue for the Ravens was avoiding the cut blocks the Broncos' offensive line is so famous for delivering.

"We were on the ground at times," said defensive tackle Sam Adams, "but when you get knocked on the ground, you have to get up quickly and be able to make some plays."

The Ravens negated the Broncos' run-blocking technique with their athleticism, said defensive end Rob Burnett.

"We said this was the best matchup in the game because we are so athletic," said Burnett, who had one of the Ravens' five sacks. "The coaches told us to stay on our feet and run to the ball."

The Ravens won that matchup and more. With what was essentially a four-man pass rush, they pressured quarterback Gus Frerotte into a 13-for-28 performance that produced 124 yards and one interception. Frerotte, playing in place of injured Brian Griese, was intercepted by middle linebacker Ray Lewis in the first quarter, Frerotte's first pick in 88 throws.

Frerotte was also unable to take advantage of the spread formation that had tormented the Ravens twice

Immaculate deflection

John Makely

Shannon Sharpe heads along the sideline to a 58-yard touchdown on a pass that was deflected twice before landing in Sharpe's hands.

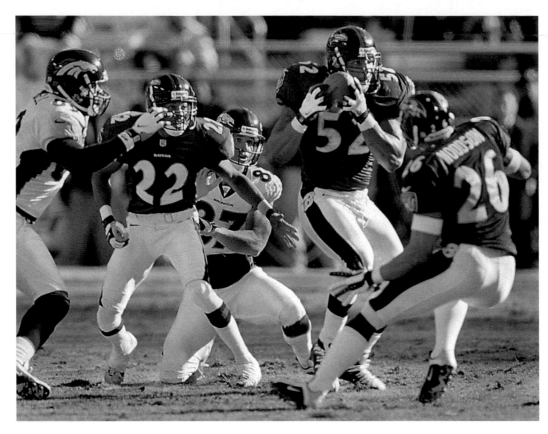

Take your pick

JOHN MAKELY

Ray Lewis intercepts a pass
by Gus Frerotte in the first
quarter. The Ravens' pressure
on Frerotte helped contain
Denver's passing game.

in the past four games.

"When we see them spread out with no running backs in the backfield, it's important to get as far up-field as we can, so he can't see receivers," Adams said.

Defense and special teams gave the Ravens' offense field position most of the day. Baltimore's average starting point was its 42-yard line. Denver's average drive started on its 23.

Offensively, the Ravens got a big rushing game from rookie running back Jamal Lewis (110 yards on 30 carries with two touchdowns) and a fortuitous touchdown pass from Trent Dilfer to tight end Shannon Sharpe, another former Bronco.

Lewis had capped a 75-yard drive with an acrobatic, 1-yard touchdown dive in the second quarter. Denver answered with Elam's field goal.

After a short, high kickoff into the wind and a 15-yard return by Corey Harris, the Ravens took over on their own 42. The game turned dramatically on the next play. It started as a short toss to Lewis in the flat. But Lewis mishandled the ball, and then Denver cornerback Terrell Buckley batted it. Sharpe, who cut short his route, wound up catching the ball when he was preparing to make a tackle.

Sharpe scampered 58 yards down the

right sideline, getting big blocks from Sam Gash and Patrick Johnson, to a huge touchdown and 14-3 lead.

The Ravens iced the game in the third quarter when a 17-yard punt return by Jermaine Lewis set them up at the Denver 28. Two plays later, Jamal Lewis bounced off middle linebacker Al Wilson and ran through would-be tackles by safeties Billy Jenkins (high) and Eric Brown (low) for a 27-yard touchdown.

Dilfer, who completed nine of 14 passes for 130 yards, left for one series in the third quarter with a concussion on a sack by Jenkins, but returned later.

The next stop for the Ravens is Tennessee, which went to the Super Bowl a year ago as a wild-card team out of the AFC Central.

"We could play them tomorrow," safety Rod Woodson said. "We could play them in the parking lot. We've been underdogs all year. We know how good we are."

Denver coach Mike Shanahan didn't offer any coronations of the Ravens' defense yet, but he did offer some perspective.

"When you win Super Bowls, I think you always put those defenses in an elite class," he said. "If Baltimore can do that, I think this defense will be considered one of the best of all time."

Over the top

Doug Kapustin

Jamal Lewis gets over a pile and gets the ball over the goal line for the Ravens' first touchdown.

103

Defensive muscle

KARL MERTON
FERRON

Rob Burnett celebrates his sack of Gus Frerotte with a little flexing for the home fans.

First down

DOUG KAPUSTIN

Qadry Ismail slips away from defensive back Ray Crockett to pick up a first down.

Visual aid

KARL MERTON
FERRON

Marcus Townsend
of Baltimore
shows his enthusi-
asm for the
Ravens' defense
when Ray Lewis is
introduced before
the game.

Pinball

DOUG KAPUSTIN

Would-be tackler Billy Jenkins bounces
off Jamal Lewis on a third-quarter
touchdown run.

Leg wrap

KARL MERTON FERRON

Michael McCrary takes the low road to sack Gus Frerotte as Keith Washington (93) also closes on the Broncos quarterback.

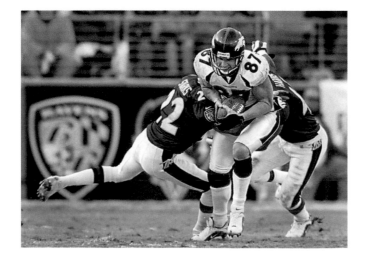

Receiver sandwich

KARL MERTON FERRON

Duane Starks (left) and Corey Harris combine to stop Broncos receiver Ed McCaffrey.

Big splash

John Makely

Rob Burnett and Tony Siragusa (hidden) douse coach Brian Billick (below) in celebration of the wild-card victory.

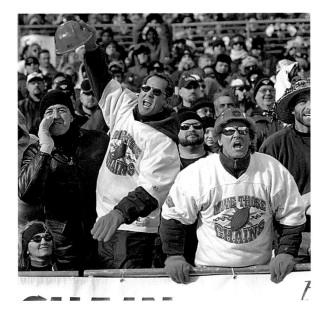

Chain gang

John Makely

Brothers Gil (left) and Jerry Sadler, in full "move those chains" regalia, don't let the cold weather chill their ardor for the Ravens.

Ravens keep riding an outrageous wave

By John Eisenberg

NASHVILLE, Tenn. — They're doing it their own way. And you couldn't dream up a more unthinkable, outrageous way if you tried. They're turning long-odds, game-winning plays into a personal art form. They're going almost nowhere on offense, yet living to tell about it. They're talking a lot of trash — too much, really — but they're backing it up.

That's the Ravens in a nutshell as they make their way through the AFC playoffs, soaring beyond even their own greatest expectations.

One win from a trip to the Super Bowl? After generating six first downs to Tennessee's 23 yesterday at Adelphia Coliseum? After winning a game that turned on, of all things, a pre-game video shown on the scoreboard and a blocked field goal returned 90 yards for a touchdown by a Raven so obscure he was wearing someone else's T-shirt underneath his jersey?

Come on, who is writing this stuff, Poe himself?

Yet Ravens coach Brian Billick was furious after his team's greatest win yesterday, feeling he'd been cheap-shotted by the Titans, who used video clips of several of his strong-talking speeches and interviews to incite the crowd before the opening kickoff. "Totally classless," Billick called the move, adding that whoever was responsible was "an idiot."

He was right. It was a low blow. And it backfired, firing up the Ravens more than the Titans, who had gained the emotional high ground after quietly listening to the Ravens' impudent crowing before the game. As the video played, the Titans lost whatever edge they'd gained.

"You saw smiles on our sideline," Ravens tight end Shannon Sharpe said. "We saw that stuff playing [on the board], and we knew we were in for a real brawl. We knew we had to back our guy up."

Of course, the Ravens had helped incite the "brawl" with their own talk, which included Patrick Johnson say-ing the Titans were "all hype," Billick predicting the winner of the Baltimore-Denver game would go to the Super Bowl and Chris McAlister saying the Titans' Eddie George had "folded like a baby" after a Ray Lewis hit the last time they played.

Such chest-beating in the face of a respectable opponent doesn't portray the image any franchise would want, and Ravens owner Art Modell reacted yesterday, saying he would demand a cooler tone from now on.

At the same time, Modell said, "we were just a supremely confident team," and indeed, talking the talk obviously is an emotional ploy that works for the Ravens, who continued to crow in the locker room after yesterday's win.

"We beat them by two touchdowns with Trent [Dilfer] playing quarterback; how bad would it have been with a good quarterback?" Sharpe said sarcastically.

Then he added: "We won here twice this year, so I guess I just foreclosed on this place." Then he turned to receiver Qadry Ismail and said, "Hey, Q, you want to buy a house?"

As furious as Billick was about the Titans' inference he has a big mouth, a team that consistently talks so boldly has to be ready to live with such accusations. Either shut up or live with the heat.

And given where they are now, in the NFL's final four, maybe they should just keep talking and live with the heat. Whatever they're doing, it's working.

"I know I felt very motivated to back up what I had said, as much as I regretted saying it once it came out," McAlister said. "That's just the way we operate."

Big talk off the field. Even bigger plays on it.

"All you can say is it must be destiny," Ravens linebacker Peter Boulware said.

Destiny? Hmmm. That's usually the straw you grasp for when you can't explain a phenomenon, but, in this case, the Ravens have a ready explanation for their sudden, dramatic rise. It's called having a defense.

Everything else about their postsea-

Unlikely hero

KARL MERTON FERRON

Little-known special
teams player Anthony
Mitchell returns a
blocked field goal 90
yards for a touchdown.

Can't hold him

<small>KENNETH K. LAM</small>

Jamal Lewis can't be kept out of the end zone by the Titans' Blaine Bishop.

son run might smack of destiny, but the defense simply refuses to budge. The Titans managed one field goal in the last 53 minutes yesterday, failing to deliver even though they controlled the ball for two-thirds of the game and started a pair of drives just 27 and 25 yards from the end zone after blocking punts.

"I say it every week and I'll say it again: Our defense is just amazing," Sharpe said.

Just as amazing but harder to fathom is everything else about the Ravens' run to the AFC championship game Sunday in Oakland.

Last week, it was the wind wreaking havoc with Denver coach Mike Shanahan's precision passing game and Sharpe grabbing the Immaculate Deflection out of the air. Yesterday, it was Tennessee kicker Al Del Greco cratering again against the Ravens, missing three of four field-goal attempts, and someone named Anthony Mitchell making the game-breaking play.

Anthony Mitchell? Wearing jersey No. 42 (and T-

shirt No. 26 under his jersey)? Go ahead, raise your hand if you knew he was a Raven before now.

Didn't think so.

OK, that's unfair. Mitchell, a safety from Tuskeegee, has performed well all season on special teams. But still, there was no reason to think he was capable of turning the tide in a playoff game until yesterday, when he grabbed a blocked field goal, turned upfield and raced 90 yards for a touchdown that broke a 10-10 tie with 12 minutes to play.

"Anthony Mitchell sums this team up," Billick said.

An unknown NFL Europe grad, hardly the proto-type for a playoff difference-maker. But the Ravens are doing it their own way, combining a lot of talk, even more defense and a penchant for the border-line miraculous.

Six first downs to 23, no running game, little passing and they're in the AFC championship game. One win from Baltimore's first Super Bowl trip in three decades. It's almost time to start casting the movie.

Punishing hit

LLOYD FOX

Ray Lewis drives quarterback Steve McNair into the turf, knocking McNair out of the game temporarily.

No-punt zone

KARL MERTON FERRON

The Titans' Chris Coleman breaks through to block Kyle Richardson's punt, the second blocked punt of the game.

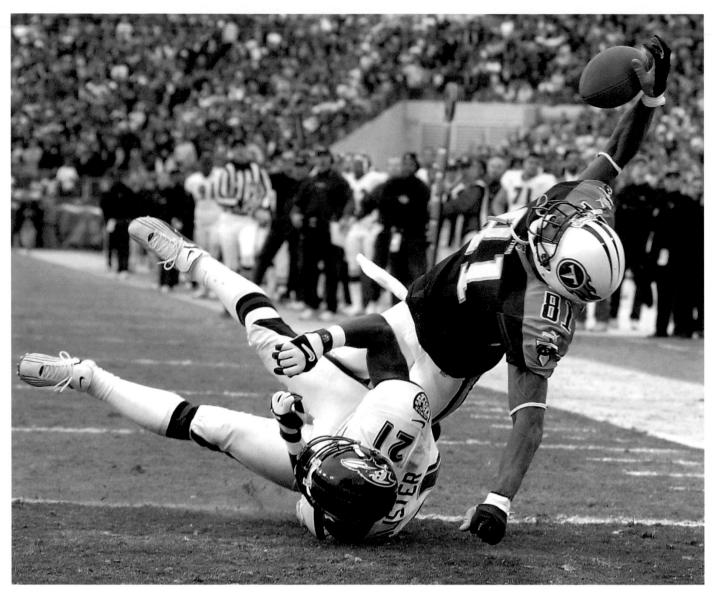

Timely play

KENNETH K. LAM

Chris McAlister hits the ground after having broken up a potential touchdown pass to Chris Sanders.

Piggyback

LLOYD FOX

Ray Lewis hops on Rod Woodson's back as they tackle Eddie George.

Take that

KENNETH K. LAM

Ravens fans Neil Quinn (left) and Bill Holland (99) savor victory. Titans fan Lori Hudspeth (right) is less enthused.

Fighting through

KARL MERTON FERRON

Keith Washington (second Raven from left) has a hand in his face and his helmet knocked off, but still gets a hand up to block Al Del Greco's field-goal try, resulting in Anthony Mitchell's touchdown runback.

Turning offensive

Doug Kapustin

Ray Lewis runs away from Frank Wycheck and the rest of the Titans with his interception for a touchdown.

The boss

Karl Merton Ferron

Owner Art Modell (left) and coach Brian Billick have lots of reason to smile: one more win and they're in the Super Bowl.

Jubilation

Lloyd Fox

Coach Brian Billick and the Ravens sideline erupts as Ray Lewis runs back an interception for a touchdown.

With Super Bowl in their grasp, Ravens apply vise

BY KEN MURRAY

OAKLAND, Calif. — With 16 seconds left in the biggest game of his life, quarterback Trent Dilfer embraced right guard Mike Flynn and let his emotions flow.

There were tears in his eyes, cameras in his face and joy in his heart.

After years of hard knocks and dry runs, Dilfer and the Ravens are going to the Super Bowl. They wrote that improbable chapter yesterday with a suffocating 16-3 victory over the Oakland Raiders in the AFC championship game at Network Associates Coliseum.

They will rendezvous with the New York Giants in Super Bowl XXXV in Tampa, Fla., in two weeks. Baltimore's first Super Bowl since 1971 will be a rematch of the NFL championship games between the Colts and Giants in 1958 and 1959.

The Giants advanced with a 41-0 romp over the Minnesota Vikings in the NFC championship game.

In a season when the Ravens have defied odds and turned a late-season winning streak into a Super Bowl run, Dilfer will go back to the site of his greatest NFL hardships. After six trying seasons with the Tampa Bay Buccaneers, he'll go back as a Super Bowl quarterback.

[8]Obviously, I'm excited," he said. "The great lesson I've learned in life is that you have to appreciate the moments in your life that are hard. You can't go running from adversity. You have to let it hit you straight in the face.

"I'm very thankful for my years in Tampa. I would not trade one single experience for anything. Those experiences helped develop the man that sits here today. I'm much more mature and much stronger than I've been."

The same could be said for the 15-4 Ravens, who will take a 10-game winning streak to Tampa. They followed their script perfectly yesterday, getting a mix of dominating defense and timely offense.

Baltimore's vise-like defense held Oakland's league-leading running game to a paltry 24 rushing yards on 17 carries. It squeezed five turnovers out of a Raiders offense that had the second-fewest giveaways in the NFL this season.

And it rendered quarterback Rich Gannon injured and ineffective after two hits by defensive end Michael McCrary and defensive tackle Tony Siragusa sent him to the sideline for a critical second-quarter stretch.

"We've got one more challenge," said defensive coordinator Marvin Lewis. "They want to make their mark in history. I've never seen so many people so resilient, so confident in each other."

The Ravens' formula may not be pretty, but it is effective. They get enough plays from the offense — they got a postseason record 96-yard touchdown pass against the Raiders — to complement a defense for the ages.

"Can defense win the Super Bowl? Damn right defense can win the Super Bowl," Siragusa said. "But you can't count our offense out. They made big plays today."

The biggest offensive play stunned the Raiders just when they had gained field position and momentum in the second quarter.

A booming 54-yard punt by Shane Lechler and a sack of Dilfer by William Thomas pinned the Ravens on their own 4 early in the period. On third-and-18, the Ravens called Rip Double Slant, ostensibly to get out of the hole. They got much more than that when Oakland showed blitz and tight end Shannon Sharpe became Dilfer's hot read.

Sharpe, lined up in the right slot, ran a slant in front of strong safety Marquez Pope. Curiously, Pope seemed to drop off Sharpe when he made the catch. Then, getting big blocks from wide receivers Brandon Stokley and Patrick Johnson, Sharpe dodged one more tackle and ran down the middle of the field.

Ninety-six yards later, the Ravens had the lead and Dilfer and Sharpe owned the NFL playoff record for longest pass.

On a raid

KARL MERTON
FERRON

Michael
McCrary rides
down quarter-
back Rich
Gannon for a
first-quarter
sack.

"They blitzed us and brought Marquez Pope on Shannon," Dilfer said. "It was supposed to work the other way. We hit it, and he did the rest. I just ran down the field, praying he got to the end zone.

"We were just trying to get out of the hole. When they decided to blitz us, we welcomed it."

The game turned dramatically, and decisively, on the Raiders' first play of their next possession. Just after Gannon launched an incomplete pass toward James Jett, he was leveled by Siragusa, whose 350-pound torso landed on the quarterback's upper body.

"I came down on him with all my weight," Siragusa said. "He screamed a little bit. I knew he was hurt once I fell on him."

Gannon, who went to the locker room to have his left shoulder examined, said he actually hurt the shoulder on a first-series sack by McCrary.

"That's when I first hurt the shoulder, and I reaggravated it on the other one," said Gannon.

Two plays later, backup quarterback Bobby Hoying missed intended receiver Jett badly, and found corner-back Duane Starks instead. Starks, who would get a second interception in the third quarter, returned it 9 yards to the Oakland 20. The Ravens got as close as the 13, where Matt Stover hit a 31-yard field goal for a 10-0 lead.

Gannon returned in the second half and played four series — enough time to get the Raiders back in the game briefly. But he was ineffective and left after committing two more turnovers.

Dilfer ended a streak of 63 consecutive passes without an interception when he opened the second half with one.

Safety Johnnie Harris picked off a pass intended for Sharpe to give Oakland the ball at the Baltimore 39— the Raiders' first foray across midfield. Gannon's 15-yard completion to tight end Jeremy Brigham and a 12-yard roughing-the-passer penalty on McCrary put the Raiders in scoring position.

But after Oakland got a first down at the 2, the Ravens delivered a goal-line stand that ended with a 24-yard Sebastian Janikowski field goal.

Defensive tackles Lional Dalton and Sam Adams stopped Tyrone Wheatley for a loss of 1 yard on first down. Linebacker Jamie Sharper sacked Gannon from behind on second down, and Gannon threw behind running back Randy Jordan on third down.

Stover added a 28-yard field goal in the third quarter after Dilfer hit Stokley (13 yards) and Ben Coates (24) for first-down passes. That made it 13-3.

It went to 16-3 when Stover kicked a 21-yarder in the fourth quarter. When Sharper intercepted Hoying at the Ravens' 2 with 3:41 left, it removed the Raiders' last hope. Dilfer completed nine of 18 passes for 190 yards, his biggest passing total since he threw for 242 on Nov. 19 in a rout of the Dallas Cowboys. He accepts his role without complaint.

"I've got no problem playing second fiddle to our defense," he said. "We do things that make us better. We were second in the league in time of possession. We have a ton of explosive plays. We were best in the league in turnover ratio.

"My teammates carried me. I don't know how good I am, but I'm the best quarterback for this team right now."

Hurting

<small>KENNETH K. LAM</small>

Rich Gannon
shows the effects
of a pounding by
300-pound-plus
Tony Siragusa.

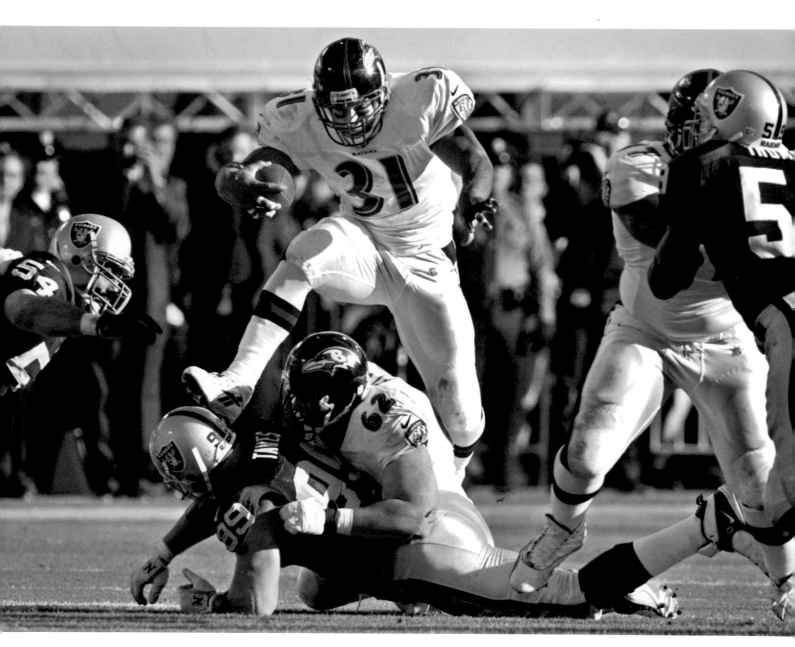

Getting over

<small>LLOYD FOX</small>

Jamal Lewis hurdles his way for
yardage in the third quarter.

Long way

GENE SWEENEY JR.

With Patrick Johnson
(83) shielding off
defenders, Shannon
Sharpe completes a
96-yard touchdown –
the longest playoff
pass in NFL history.

Coming through

GENE SWEENEY JR.

Tony Siragusa is about to land on Rich Gannon, sending him to the sideline.

Agony and defeat

LLOYD FOX

Rich Gannon (14), Bobby Hoying and coach Jon Gruden look distraught as the Raiders' loss sinks in.

Defensive line-up

LLOYD FOX

Defensive linemen Adalius Thomas, Michael McCrary, Tony Siragusa, Lional Dalton and Rob Burnett (from left) gather around the conference championship trophy.

Tampa-bound

JOHN MAKELY

Qadry Ismail celebrates amid confetti after the Ravens earn a trip to the Super Bowl.

At last

GENE SWEENEY JR.

Art Modell can't hide his satisfaction at finally making the Super Bowl as his players hoist the AFC championship trophy.

Purple Reign

BY KEN MURRAY

TAMPA, Fla. — Now there can be no doubt.

The Ravens claimed their place in history last night with one final dissertation on great defense.

A team that swaggered into Super Bowl XXXV delivered on its sound and fury of the past week with a 34-7 demolition of the New York Giants before 71,921 at Raymond James Stadium.

It was the crowning glory, and defining moment, of a season that produced Baltimore's first Super Bowl championship in 30 years, since the Colts beat the Dallas Cowboys, 16-13, in Super Bowl V in 1971.

Collecting four interceptions against overmatched quarterback Kerry Collins, the wild-card Ravens (16-4) completed the improbable turnaround from perennial losers to Super Bowl champions in only coach Brian Billick's second season.

Their 11th straight victory followed a formula that proved unbeatable down the stretch: suffocating defense, opportunistic special teams and a timely play on offense.

They got a 38-yard touchdown pass from quarterback Trent Dilfer to Brandon Stokley for the early lead, an 84-yard kickoff return for a clinching touchdown and an MVP performance from team leader and middle linebacker Ray Lewis.

Lewis had five tackles and deflected four passes to become the seventh defensive player in the history of the Super Bowl — and first middle linebacker — to win the Pete Rozelle Award as MVP.

"It was amazing the way we came out," Lewis said. "I mean, it was incredible to see the way we came out and played as a team. This defense has been doing this all year, and never, never got the credit.

"This win is something they can't take away from us. We are the best ever, the best ever right now."

The triumph completed Lewis' journey back from infamy. After last season's Super Bowl in Atlanta, he was charged in a double murder and had to undergo a high-profile trial. Even after the charges were dropped in a plea bargain agreement in exchange for an obstruction of justice misdemeanor charge, Lewis had the cloud of suspicion over him.

Yesterday, Lewis dominated play in the first half when the Ravens grabbed a 10-0 lead they would not relinquish.

"He has a way of always setting the tone," said defensive coordinator Marvin Lewis.

"He sets the tone when he comes out of that tunnel. He's been that way from the very first day he walked into that building. He's set the tone for this organization. He's a quality person, a quality player, and you see everyone feed off of it."

The Ravens' defense backed up a week of bravado that had several players calling for a shutout and their rightful place among the best defenses in NFL history.

The Ravens didn't get the shutout — New York's Ron Dixon returned a kickoff for a 97-yard touchdown in the third quarter — even though they deserved one.

Baltimore's defense allowed the Giants just 33 total yards in the second half, and 152 for the game. The Giants were only 2-for-14 on third down.

In their four-game Super Bowl run, the Ravens' defense gave up just one touchdown, and the team outscored its opponents by a combined 95-23.

"This is the best defense ever to play the game," said defensive tackle Tony Siragusa.

The Ravens had a field day at Collins' expense. A Ray Lewis deflection turned into an interception by linebacker Jamie Sharper in the second quarter. Cornerback Chris McAlister snuffed the Giants' best scoring threat with an interception at the Ravens' 1-yard line at the end of the first half.

Safety Kim Herring had a third-quarter interception, and when cornerback Duane Starks added a fourth, the game turned decisively.

Starks jumped in front of intended receiver Amani Toomer to steal a Collins' pass, and then ran untouched to the end zone for a 49-yard touchdown with 3:49 left in the third quarter.

Collins completed 15 of 39 passes for 112 yards, and tied a Super Bowl record with his four interceptions.

He was asked if he had ever seen a better defense.

"No, probably not," Collins said. "This is a good defense. They have good players, and they're coached very well.

"That's one of the things that jump out, just how well-coached they are and well-disciplined they are. They play together very well. They completely took me out of my rhythm. Everything I tried

Inspiring

KARL MERTON FERRON

Jermaine Lewis points skyward after running back a kickoff for an 84-yard touchdown.

125

Just the beginning

JOHN MAKELY

Some might have thought this pre-game show would be the only fireworks at the Super Bowl.

to get going always seemed to end up in a bad stop."

Starks said he knew the route was coming from studying video of Collins.

"I studied his three-step drop," he said. "When he gave me that little extra hop, I knew he was going to throw the ball. I had a positive read, I knew I had the upper hand on that three-step read."

In the space of 36 seconds and 21 points — starting with that interception — the Ravens lost their shutout, but put the game away.

Dixon returned the ensuing kickoff for New York's only touchdown of the night. Cornell Brown was the only player who got a hand on Dixon, who outran kicker Matt Stover at midfield.

At 17-7, the Giants had hope.

But not for long.

Jermaine Lewis returned the next kickoff 84 yards for a touchdown. They were the first back-to-back kickoff return touchdowns in Super Bowl history.

Lewis got big blocks from Corey Harris and Sam Gash to go down the right sideline.

The Ravens' offense contributed a fourth-quarter touchdown drive that covered 38 yards and ended with a 3-yard run by Jamal Lewis.

Stover kicked field goals of 47 and 34 yards, and was wide left on a 41-yard try in the third quarter.

Dilfer completed 12 of 25 passes for 153 yards and no turnovers, although he had one interception returned for a touchdown that was wiped out by a penalty call against the Giants.

His 38-yard strike to Stokley in the first quarter was on a perfectly thrown pass.

"We knew if we got the lead, it was going to be a hard day for them," Dilfer said.

"We have the best defense in the history of the universe. And it's fine that some of these old coaches and old players want to argue for their [defenses]. They should.

"But this is just proof. Our defense has proven it time after time after time. We're a great football team because we play to our strengths."

The victory was especially rewarding for Dilfer because he spent six years with the Tampa Bay Buccaneers before joining the Ravens last off-season as a free agent.

It was also the third Super Bowl victory in four years for tight end Shannon Sharpe, another off-season free-agent acquisition. "This one is incredible, because nobody thought that we could do it," Sharpe said.

"Nobody picked us to get this far. We came out of nowhere. The guys in the locker room believed we could do it. I don't think many people thought we could even get it done today.

"My hat is off to our defense. What a job they did today."

D man

LLOYD FOX

Rob Burnett stands over fallen Kerry Collins after sacking him in the first quarter.

Just in

KENNETH K. LAM

As Cornelius Griffin knocks him out of bounds, Jamal Lewis holds on to the ball just long enough to get it over the goal line for a touchdown.

Breaking the ice

LLOYD FOX

Brandon Stokley, in the
grasp of Jason Sehorn, has
a reception for the first
touchdown of the game.

Worth
the trip

KARL MERTON
FERRON

Plenty of Ravens
fans made it to
Tampa, and they
obviously were
enjoying the game.

Higher and higher

GENE SWEENEY JR.

Jeff Mitchell gives Trent Dilfer a lift, just as Dilfer's touchdown pass to Brandon Stokley lifted the Ravens.

129

Most valuable

GENE SWEENEY JR.

Ray Lewis exhorts his teammates and the crowd after a tackle. Lewis was named Super Bowl MVP.

Snuffed

KENNETH K. LAM

Chris McAlister (left) exults in his interception near the goal line that shut off a Giants scoring opportunity.

A good tip

LLOYD FOX

Jamie Sharper cradles an interception of a ball tipped by Ray Lewis.

Winning couple

KENNETH K. LAM

Center Jeff Mitchell shares his victorious Super Bowl moment on the field with his wife, Christine.

Trophy coach

LLOYD FOX

Brian Billick shows off the hardware: the Vince Lombardi Trophy.

Sharing the joy

KENNETH K. LAM

A woman helped from the stands by Brandon Stokley dances amid the confetti.

This is it

GENE SWEENEY JR.

The joy of winning
a Super Bowl is
written all over
Jermaine Lewis'
face.

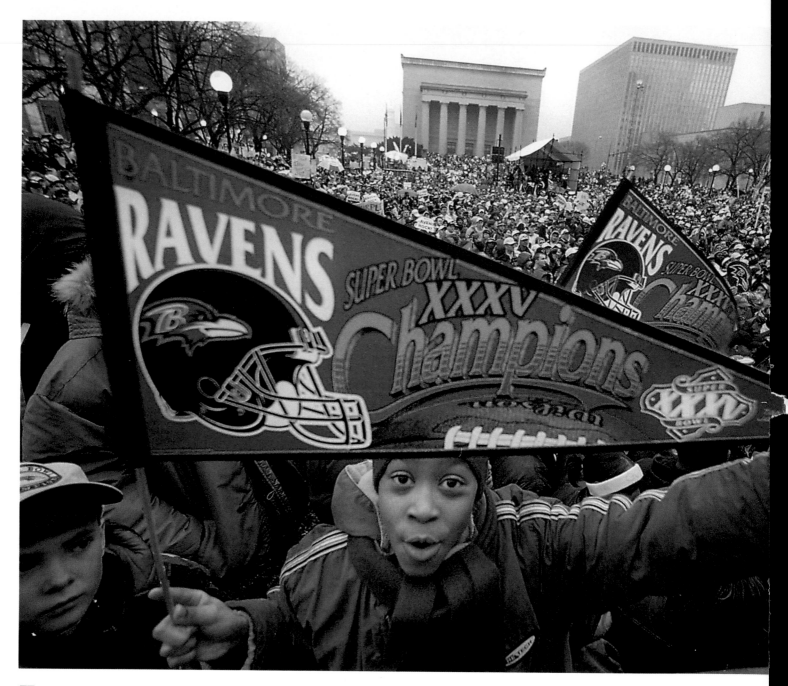

Her team

JED KIRSCHBAUM

Jasmine Berry, 10, of Baltimore epitomizes the sentiments of the crowd at the Ravens' victory parade downtown.

Hummin' along

PERRY THORSVIK

Ravens players ride through the wet streets in a caravan of Humvees.

Hail to the QB

DAVID HOBBY

Trent Dilfer acknowledges the cheers of the crowd during player introductions at City Hall.

His prizes

DAVID HOBBY

With daughter Samantha on his shoulders, Tony Siragusa hoists the Lombardi Trophy high as Mayor Martin O'Malley (far left) looks on.

Statistics

The following game-by-game statistics were furnished by The Sports Network.

Ravens vs. Steelers

SCORE BY QUARTERS

TEAM	1	2	3	4	OT	SCORE
Baltimore	10	3	3	0		16
Pittsburgh	0	0	0	0		0

SCORING SUMMARY

1st Quarter — Baltimore Field Goal - 23-yarder by Matt Stover. 6:50 remaining. (3 plays, 8 yards. Time of Drive: 1:41).
Baltimore Touchdown - 53-yard pass from Tony Banks to Qadry Ismail. (Matt Stover kick). 3:58 remaining. (1 play, 53 yards. Time of Drive: 0:15).
2nd Quarter — Baltimore Field Goal - 26-yarder by Matt Stover. 0:00 remaining. (15 plays, 66 yards. Time of Drive: 6:57).
3rd Quarter — Baltimore Field Goal - 33-yarder by Matt Stover. 11:31 remaining. (8 plays, 36 yards. Time of Drive: 3:29).
4th Quarter — No scoring.

FINAL TEAM STATISTICS

	Baltimore	Pittsburgh
First Downs	18	12
Rushes-Yards	36-140	18-30
Passing Yards	196	193
Return Yards	88	48
Passing (Att-Comp-Int)	32-18-0	39-17-0
Punts-Average	7-40.1	6-50.8
Sacked-Yards Lost	1-3	1-6
Fumbles-Lost	0-0	3-1
Penalties-Yards	6-42	2-15
Time of Possession	35:07	24:53

Ravens vs. Jaguars

SCORE BY QUARTERS

TEAM	1	2	3	4	OT	SCORE
Jacksonville	17	6	3	10		36
Baltimore	0	7	15	17		39

SCORING SUMMARY

1st Quarter — Jacksonville Field Goal - 35-yarder by Mike Hollis. 11:15 remaining. (7 plays, 48 yards. Time of Drive: 3:45). Jacksonville Touchdown - 45-yard pass from Mark Brunell to Jimmy Smith. (Mike Hollis kick). 7:49 remaining. (4 plays, 43 yards. Time of Drive: 1:32). Jacksonville Touchdown - 43-yard pass from Mark Brunell to Jimmy Smith. (Mike Hollis kick). 2:32 remaining. (5 plays, 77 yards. Time of Drive: 2:47).
2nd Quarter — Baltimore Touchdown - 14-yard pass from Tony Banks to Travis Taylor. (Matt Stover kick). 14:48 remaining. (1 play, 14 yards. Time of Drive: 0:06). Jacksonville Field Goal - 45-yarder by Mike Hollis. 3:36 remaining. (14 plays, 63 yards. Time of Drive: 6:40). Jacksonville Field Goal - 48-yarder by Mike Hollis. 0:44 remaining. (8 plays, 28 yards. Time of Drive: 0:58).
3rd Quarter — Baltimore Touchdown - 22-yard pass from Tony Banks to Travis Taylor. (Tony Banks pass to Ben Coates). 13:31 remaining. (4 plays, 68 yards. Time of Drive: 1:29). Jacksonville Field Goal - 34-yarder by Mike Hollis. 6:47 remaining. (9 plays, 25 yards. Time of Drive: 4:54). Baltimore Touchdown - 5-yard pass from Tony Banks to Obafemi Ayanbadejo. (Matt Stover kick). 1:02 remaining. (10 plays, 76 yards. Time of Drive: 5:45).
4th Quarter — Baltimore Touchdown - 12-yard pass from Tony Banks to Jermaine Lewis. (Matt Stover kick). 10:00 remaining. (2 plays, 12 yards. Time of Drive: 0:09). Baltimore Field Goal - 44-yarder by Matt Stover. 7:00 remaining. (4 plays, 9 yards. Time of Drive: 1:28). Jacksonville Field Goal - 48-yarder by Mike Hollis. 3:53 remaining. (9 plays, 51 yards. Time of Drive: 3:07). Jacksonville Touchdown - 40-yard pass from Mark Brunell to Jimmy Smith. (Mike Hollis kick). 1:45 remaining. (4 plays, 61 yards. Time of Drive: 1:08). Baltimore Touchdown - 29-yard pass from Tony Banks to Shannon Sharpe. (Matt Stover kick). 0:41 remaining. (7 plays, 75 yards. Time of Drive: 1:04).

FINAL TEAM STATISTICS

	Jacksonville	Baltimore
First Downs	22	17
Rushes-Yards	21-46	18-89
Passing Yards	375	242
Return Yards	62	32
Passing (Att-Comp-Int)	50-28-2	40-23-2
Punts-Average	3-38.0	7-41.1
Fumbles-Lost	4-2	1-0
Penalties-Yards	10-60	8-65
Time of Possession	31:23	28:37

Ravens vs. Dolphins

SCORE BY QUARTERS

TEAM	1	2	3	4	OT	SCORE
Baltimore	0	0	3	3		6
Miami	3	3	7	6		19

SCORING SUMMARY

1st Quarter — Miami Field Goal - 42-yarder by Olindo Mare. 4:55 remaining. (10 plays, 47 yards. Time of Drive: 6:29).
2nd Quarter — Miami Field Goal - 41-yarder by Olindo Mare. 12:37 remaining. (9 plays, 25 yards. Time of Drive: 4:46).
3rd Quarter — Miami Touchdown - 7-yard run by Lamar Smith. (Olindo Mare kick). 11:47 remaining. (5 plays, 61 yards. Time of Drive: 3:13).
Baltimore Field Goal - 27-yarder by Matt Stover. 3:13 remaining. (13 plays, 67 yards. Time of Drive: 8:34).
4th Quarter — Miami Touchdown - 8-yard pass from Jay Fiedler to Lamar Smith. (kick failed). 13:15 remaining. (8 plays, 80 yards. Time of Drive: 4:58).
Baltimore Field Goal - 33-yarder by Matt Stover. 9:35 remaining. (8 plays, 55 yards. Time of Drive: 3:40).

FINAL TEAM STATISTICS

	Baltimore	Miami
First Downs	18	15
Rushes-Yards	18-118	34-106
Passing Yards	144	152
Return Yards	99	144
Passing (Att-Comp-Int)	31-19-1	16-11-1
Punts-Average	4-41.0	3-48.3
Fumbles-Lost	3-0	0-0
Penalties-Yards	4-20	6-38
Time of Possession	28:49	31:11

Ravens vs. Bengals

SCORE BY QUARTERS

TEAM	1	2	3	4	OT	SCORE
Cincinnati	0	0	0	0		0
Baltimore	10	14	3	10		37

SCORING SUMMARY

1st Quarter — Baltimore Field Goal - 30-yarder by Matt Stover. 8:38 remaining. (11 plays, 50 yards. Time of Drive: 6:22).
Baltimore Touchdown - 8-yard pass from Tony Banks to Travis Taylor. (Matt Stover kick). 0:50 remaining. (10 plays, 62 yards. Time of Drive: 5:26).
2nd Quarter — Baltimore Touchdown - 11-yard run by Jamal Lewis. (Matt Stover kick). 14:56 remaining. (3 plays, 27 yards. Time of Drive: 0:44).
Baltimore Touchdown - 1-yard pass from Tony Banks to Shannon Sharpe. (Matt Stover kick). 3:05 remaining. (10 plays, 44 yards. Time of Drive: 4:53).
3rd Quarter — Baltimore Field Goal - 37-yarder by Matt Stover. 3:03 remaining. (13 plays, 27 yards. Time of Drive: 6:36).
4th Quarter — Baltimore Touchdown - 1-yard run by Obafemi Ayanbadejo. (Matt Stover kick). 6:39 remaining. (11 plays, 66 yards. Time of Drive: 4:51).
Baltimore Field Goal - 19-yarder by Matt Stover. 1:57 remaining. (8 plays, 40 yards. Time of Drive: 3:30).

FINAL TEAM STATISTICS

	Cincinnati	Baltimore
First Downs	7	27
Rushes-Yards	16-4	38-176
Passing Yards	90	215
Return Yards	156	65
Passing (Att-Comp-Int)	24-15-2	39-22-0
Punts-Average	4-36.5	1-33.0
Fumbles-Lost	2-2	1-1
Penalties-Yards	8-53	10-90
Time of Possession	21:16	38:44

Ravens vs. Browns

SCORE BY QUARTERS

TEAM	1	2	3	4	OT	SCORE
Baltimore	3	6	3	0		12
Cleveland	0	0	0	0		0

SCORING SUMMARY

1st Quarter — Baltimore Field Goal - 45-yarder by Matt Stover. 6:57 remaining. (5 plays, 23 yards. Time of Drive: 2:54).
2nd Quarter — Baltimore Field Goal - 30-yarder by Matt Stover. 11:30 remaining. (11 plays, 50 yards. Time of Drive: 6:05).
Baltimore Field Goal - 44-yarder by Matt Stover. 9:12 remaining. (4 plays, 5 yards. Time of Drive: 1:57).
3rd Quarter — Baltimore Field Goal - 22-yarder by Matt Stover. 4:56 remaining. (19 plays, 76 yards. Time of Drive: 9:56).

4th Quarter — No scoring.

FINAL TEAM STATISTICS

	Baltimore	Cleveland
First Downs	22	11
Rushes-Yards	37-188	13-23
Passing Yards	160	207
Return Yards	79	16
Passing (Att-Comp-Int)	34-18-1	36-21-3
Punts-Average	3-42.7	4-50.8
Fumbles-Lost	0-0	3-1
Penalties-Yards	6-62	8-60
Time of Possession	36:44	23:16

Ravens vs. Jaguars

SCORE BY QUARTERS

TEAM	1	2	3	4	OT	SCORE
Baltimore	3	3	3	6		15
Jacksonville	3	0	0	7		10

SCORING SUMMARY

1st Quarter — Jacksonville Field Goal - 49-yarder by Steve Lindsey. 8:04 remaining. (4 plays, 2 yards. Time of Drive: 0:56).
Baltimore Field Goal - 47-yarder by Matt Stover. 1:23 remaining. (6 plays, 34 yards. Time of Drive: 2:24).
2nd Quarter — Baltimore Field Goal - 32-yarder by Matt Stover. 0:21 remaining. (5 plays, 18 yards. Time of Drive: 0:42).
3rd Quarter — Baltimore Field Goal - 43-yarder by Matt Stover. 12:37 remaining. (4 plays, (-1) yards. Time of Drive: 1:35).
4th Quarter — Baltimore Field Goal - 21-yarder by Matt Stover. 13:38 remaining. (16 plays, 65 yards. Time of Drive: 7:24). Baltimore Field Goal - 24-yarder by Matt Stover. 9:44 remaining. (3 plays, (-4) yards. Time of Drive: 1:11). Jacksonville Touchdown - 1-yard run by Fred Taylor. (Steve Lindsey kick). 4:04 remaining. (13 plays, 75 yards. Time of Drive: 5:40).

FINAL TEAM STATISTICS

	Baltimore	Jacksonville
First Downs	10	22
Rushes-Yards	25-56	27-95
Passing Yards	138	253
Return Yards	111	40
Passing (Att-Comp-Int)	17-39-0	29-43-3
Punts-Average	9-41.9	5-38.0
Fumbles-Lost	1-1	8-3
Penalties-Yards	5-25	6-34
Time of Possession	28:12	31:48

Ravens vs. Redskins

SCORE BY QUARTERS

TEAM	1	2	3	4	OT	SCORE
Baltimore	0	3	0	0		3
Washington	0	3	0	7		10

SCORING SUMMARY

1st Quarter — No scoring.
2nd Quarter — Washington Field Goal - 37-yarder by Kris Heppner. 7:45 remaining. (11 plays, 45 yards. Time of Drive: 6:21).
Baltimore Field Goal - 51-yarder by Matt Stover. 3:14 remaining. (9 plays, 28 yards. Time of Drive: 4:31).
3rd Quarter — No scoring.
4th Quarter — Washington Touchdown - 33-yard run by Stephen Davis. (Kris Heppner kick). 14:18 remaining. (7 plays, 80 yards. Time of Drive: 3:16).

FINAL TEAM STATISTICS

	Baltimore	Washington
First Downs	15	15
Rushes-Yards	25-91	29-101
Passing Yards	108	145
Return Yards	20	23
Passing (Att-Comp-Int)	27-16-1	27-18-1
Punts-Average	7-40.4	4-42.0
Fumbles-Lost	0-0	1-1
Penalties-Yards	7-41	6-51
Time of Possession	31:04	28:56

Ravens vs. Titans

SCORE BY QUARTERS

TEAM	1	2	3	4	OT	SCORE
Tennessee	0	7	7	0		14
Baltimore	3	3	0	0		6

SCORING SUMMARY

1st Quarter — Baltimore Field Goal - 21-yarder by Matt Stover. 5:04 remaining. (12 plays, 57 yards. Time of Drive: 6:11).

2nd Quarter — Baltimore Field Goal - 38-yarder by Matt Stover. 10:44 remaining. (15 plays, 77 yards. Time of Drive: 6:47). Tennessee Touchdown - 9-yard pass from Steve McNair to Rodney Thomas. (Al Del Greco kick). 0:44 remaining. (5 plays, 38 yards. Time of Drive: 0:54).
3rd Quarter — Tennessee Touchdown - 24-yard interception return by Randall Godfrey. (Al Del Greco kick). 13:22 remaining.
4th Quarter — No scoring.

FINAL TEAM STATISTICS

	Tennessee	Baltimore
First Downs	7	24
Rushes-Yards	26-90	29-113
Passing Yards	101	255
Return Yards	63	30
Passing (Att-Comp-Int)	21-11-1	46-25-4
Punts-Average	7-45.9	5-36.8
Fumbles-Lost	2-1	7-0
Penalties-Yards	4-20	8-52
Time of Possession	23:59	36:01

Ravens vs. Steelers

SCORE BY QUARTERS

TEAM	1	2	3	4	OT	SCORE
Pittsburgh	0	0	9	0		9
Baltimore	0	6	0	0		6

SCORING SUMMARY

1st Quarter — No scoring.
2nd Quarter — Baltimore Field Goal - 51-yarder by Matt Stover. 11:20 remaining. (6 plays, 33 yards. Time of Drive: 2:54). Baltimore Field Goal - 49-yarder by Matt Stover. 1:52 remaining. (9 plays, 49 yards. Time of Drive: 4:19).
3rd Quarter — Pittsburgh Touchdown - 45-yard pass from Kordell Stewart to Hines Ward. (kick failed). 9:51 remaining. (2 plays, 59 yards. Time of Drive: 0:50). Pittsburgh Field Goal - 24-yarder by Kris Brown. 5:54 remaining. (6 plays, 21 yards. Time of Drive: 3:48).
4th Quarter — No scoring.

FINAL TEAM STATISTICS

	Pittsburgh	Baltimore
First Downs	14	14
Rushes-Yards	34-120	28-135
Passing Yards	111	139
Return Yards	0	27
Passing (Att-Comp-Int)	18-9-0	24-11-1
Punts-Average	7-39.7	4-32.0
Fumbles-Lost	2-1	2-2
Penalties-Yards	3-20	4-20
Time of Possession	31:58	28:02

Ravens vs. Bengals

SCORE BY QUARTERS

TEAM	1	2	3	4	OT	SCORE
Baltimore	3	21	0	3		27
Cincinnati	0	0	7	0		7

SCORING SUMMARY

1st Quarter — Baltimore Field Goal - 38-yarder by Matt Stover. 2:28 remaining. (7 plays, 48 yards. Time of Drive: 3:30).
2nd Quarter — Baltimore Touchdown - 14-yard pass from Trent Dilfer to Brandon Stokley. (Matt Stover kick). 14:07 remaining. (3 plays, 16 yards. Time of Drive: 0:55). Baltimore Touchdown - 18-yard pass from Trent Dilfer to Shannon Sharpe. (Matt Stover kick). 6:25 remaining. (11 plays, 80 yards. Time of Drive: 4:55). Baltimore Touchdown - 19-yard pass from Trent Dilfer to Shannon Sharpe. (Matt Stover kick). 2:04 remaining. (4 plays, 69 yards. Time of Drive: 2:04).
3rd Quarter — Cincinnati Touchdown - 4-yard run by Peter Warrick. (Neil Rackers kick). 6:13 remaining. (6 plays, 15 yards. Time of Drive: 2:30).
4th Quarter — Baltimore Field Goal - 32-yarder by Matt Stover. 8:58 remaining. (7 plays, 23 yards. Time of Drive: 3:20).

FINAL TEAM STATISTICS

	Baltimore	Cincinnati
First Downs	19	11
Rushes-Yards	31-142	27-44
Passing Yards	236	130
Return Yards	54	187
Passing (Att-Comp-Int)	34-23-1	27-15-0
Punts-Average	6-41.0	8-43.4
Fumbles-Lost	0-0	2-1
Penalties-Yards	6-50	6-40
Time of Possession	33:13	26:47

Ravens vs. Titans

SCORE BY QUARTERS

TEAM	1	2	3	4	OT	SCORE
Baltimore	7	10	0	7		24
Tennessee	0	14	0	9		23

SCORING SUMMARY

1st Quarter — Baltimore Touchdown - 46-yard pass from Trent Dilfer to Qadry Ismail. (Matt Stover kick). 9:58 remaining. (5 plays, 63 yards. Time of Drive: 1:57).
2nd Quarter — Baltimore Touchdown - 2-yard run by Jamal Lewis. (Matt Stover kick). 12:26 remaining. (17 plays, 96 yards. Time of Drive: 10:11). Tennessee Touchdown - 10-yard pass from Steve McNair to Derrick Mason. (Al Del Greco kick). 8:10 remaining. (9 plays, 63 yards. Time of Drive: 4:16). Baltimore Field Goal - 45-yarder by Matt Stover. 1:04 remaining. (9 plays, 41 yards. Time of Drive: 3:14). Tennessee Touchdown - 4-yard pass from Steve McNair to Lorenzo Neal. (Al Del Greco kick). 0:03 remaining. (5 plays, 53 yards. Time of Drive: 1:01).
3rd Quarter — No scoring.
4th Quarter — Tennessee Field Goal - 23-yarder by Al Del Greco. 8:23 remaining. (12 plays, 86 yards. Time of Drive: 6:30). - Tennessee Touchdown - 87-yard interception return by Perry Phenix. (Kick failed). 2:30 remaining. Baltimore Touchdown - 2-yard pass from Trent Dilfer to Patrick Johnson. (Matt Stover kick). 0:25 remaining. (9 plays, 70 yards. Time of Drive: 2:05).

FINAL TEAM STATISTICS

	Baltimore	Tennessee
First Downs	19	17
Rushes-Yards	29-103	16-62
Passing Yards	258	224
Return Yards	34	102
Passing (Att-Comp-Int)	36-23-1	34-21-0
Punts-Average	6-38.3	5-49.0
Fumbles-Lost	0-0	2-2
Penalties-Yards	8-72	8-64
Time of Possession	34:14	25:46

Ravens vs. Cowboys

SCORE BY QUARTERS

TEAM	1	2	3	4	OT	SCORE
Dallas	0	0	0	0		0
Baltimore	10	7	0	10		27

SCORING SUMMARY

1st Quarter — Baltimore Touchdown - 40-yard pass from Trent Dilfer to Qadry Ismail. (Matt Stover kick). 11:25 remaining. (7 plays, 81 yards. Time of Drive: 3:35). Baltimore Field Goal - 25-yarder by Matt Stover. 5:02 remaining. (9 plays, 50 yards. Time of Drive: 4:26).
2nd Quarter — Baltimore Touchdown - 59-yard pass from Trent Dilfer to Shannon Sharpe. (Matt Stover kick). 2:07 remaining. (4 plays, 71 yards. Time of Drive: 2:10).
3rd Quarter — No scoring.
4th Quarter — Baltimore Field Goal - 19-yarder by Matt Stover. 7:42 remaining. (11 plays, 53 yards. Time of Drive: 7:05). Baltimore Touchdown - 5-yard run by Priest Holmes. 3:52 remaining. (6 plays, 51 yards. Time of Drive: 2:38).

FINAL TEAM STATISTICS

	Dallas	Baltimore
First Downs	9	22
Rushes-Yards	14-55	44-250
Passing Yards	137	229
Return Yards	16	66
Passing (Att-Comp-Int)	33-19-3	24-18-2
Punts-Average	7-37.1	3-37.7
Fumbles-Lost	1-0	0-0
Penalties-Yards	3-15	6-55
Time of Possession	21:38	38:22

Ravens vs. Browns

SCORE BY QUARTERS

TEAM	1	2	3	4	OT	SCORE
Cleveland	7	0	0	0		7
Baltimore	7	24	6	7		44

SCORING SUMMARY

1st Quarter— Cleveland Touchdown - 4-yard run by Travis Prentice. (Phil Dawson kick). 10:30 remaining. (4 plays, 86 yards. Time of Drive: 1:42). Baltimore Touchdown - 1-yard run by Jamal Lewis. (Matt Stover kick). 4:06 remaining. (13 plays, 66 yards. Time of Drive: 6:24).
2nd Quarter— Baltimore Touchdown - 2-yard pass from Trent Dilfer to Sam Gash. (Matt Stover kick). 13:40 remaining. (7 plays, 44 yards. Time of Drive: 3:35). Baltimore Touchdown - 46-yard pass from Trent Dilfer to Patrick Johnson. (Matt Stover kick). 11:39 remaining. (1 play, 46 yards. Time of Drive: 0:07). Baltimore Field Goal - 39-yarder by Matt Stover. 4:35 remaining. (10 plays, 69 yards. Time of Drive: 5:13). Baltimore Touchdown - 36-yard run by Jamal Lewis. (Matt Stover kick). 2:55 remaining. (2 plays, 44 yards. Time of Drive: 0:46).
3rd Quarter— Baltimore Field Goal - 26-yarder by Matt Stover. 11:52 remaining. (5 plays, 18 yards. Time of Drive: 2:09). - Baltimore Field Goal - 38-yarder by Matt Stover. 5:01 remaining. (11 plays, 46 yards. Time of Drive: 5:01).
4th Quarter— Baltimore Touchdown - 3-yard run by Priest Holmes. (Matt Stover kick). 5:23 remaining. (3 plays, 6 yards. Time of Drive: 1:30).

FINAL TEAM STATISTICS

	Cleveland	Baltimore
First Downs	5	25
Rushes-Yards	17-28	51-247
Passing Yards	84	214
Return Yards	33	140
Passing (Att-Comp-Int)	25-13-1	26-14-1
Punts-Average	10-49.1	4-47.3
Fumbles-Lost	2-2	2-1
Penalties-Yards	3-11	3-25
Time of Possession	21:28	38:32

Ravens vs. Chargers

SCORE BY QUARTERS

TEAM	1	2	3	4	OT	SCORE
San Diego	0	3	0	0		3
Baltimore	3	7	14	0		24

SCORING SUMMARY

1st Quarter — Baltimore Field Goal - 32-yarder by Matt Stover. 3:43 remaining. (17 plays, 60 yards. Time of Drive: 9:01).
2nd Quarter — Baltimore Touchdown - 28-yard pass from Trent Dilfer to Qadry Ismail. (Matt Stover kick). 4:16 remaining. (8 plays, 46 yards. Time of Drive: 3:55). San Diego Field Goal - 47-yarder by John Carney. 0:48 remaining. (6 plays, 14 yards. Time of Drive: 1:41).
3rd Quarter — Baltimore Touchdown - 1-yard run by Jamal Lewis. (Matt Stover kick). 10:47 remaining. (2 plays, 3 yards. Time of Drive: 0:55). Baltimore Touchdown - 22-yard pass from Trent Dilfer to Brandon Stokley. (Matt Stover kick). 4:51 remaining. (3 plays, 17 yards. Time of Drive: 2:00).
4th Quarter .— No scoring.

FINAL TEAM STATISTICS

	San Diego	Baltimore
First Downs	9	19
Rushes-Yards	26-64	40-110
Passing Yards	64	166
Return Yards	29	41
Passing (Att-Comp-Int)	23-9-1	24-16-2
Punts-Average	4-45.0	3-40.0
Fumbles-Lost	5-4	2-1
Penalties-Yards	4-20	3-15
Time of Possession	22:24	37:36

Ravens vs. Cardinals

SCORE BY QUARTERS

TEAM	1	2	3	4	OT	SCORE
Baltimore	3	0	10	0		13
Arizona	0	0	7	0		7

SCORING SUMMARY

1st Quarter — Baltimore Field Goal - 42-yarder by Matt Stover. 7:12 remaining. (13 plays, 68 yards. Time of Drive: 6:13).
2nd Quarter — No scoring.
3rd Quarter — Arizona Touchdown - 27-yard pass from Jake Plummer to Frank Sanders. (Cary Blanchard kick). 9:41 remaining. (7 plays, 60 yards. Time of Drive: 2:22). Baltimore Touchdown - 1-yard run by Jamal Lewis. (Matt Stover kick). 6:17 remaining. (3 plays, 6 yards. Time of Drive: 1:31). Baltimore Field Goal - 42-yarder by Matt Stover. 0:21 remaining. (7 plays, 23 yards. Time of Drive: 3:38).
4th Quarter — No scoring.

FINAL TEAM STATISTICS

	Baltimore	Arizona
First Downs	14	18
Rushes-Yards	37-177	23-51
Passing Yards	37	258
Return Yards	134	34
Passing (Att-Comp-Int)	22-12-1	43-23-2
Punts-Average	7-38.7	4-45.3
Fumbles-Lost	3-1	3-2
Penalties-Yards	6-64	3-15
Time of Possession	31:57	28:03

Ravens vs. Jets

SCORE BY QUARTERS

TEAM	1	2	3	4	OT	SCORE
NY Jets	14	0	3	3		20
Baltimore	0	20	7	7		34

SCORING SUMMARY

1st Quarter — New York Touchdown - 37-yard pass from Vinny Testaverde to Dedric Ward. (Brett Conway kick). 12:36 remaining. (5 plays, 70 yards. Time of Drive: 2:24). New York Touchdown - 35-yard pass from Vinny Testaverde to Richie Anderson. (Brett Conway kick). 8:49 remaining. (7 plays, 70 yards. Time of Drive: 2:11).
2nd Quarter — Baltimore Touchdown - 7-yard pass from Trent Dilfer to Qadry Ismail. (Matt Stover kick). 12:07 remaining. (5 plays, 42 yards. Time of Drive 2:43). Baltimore Field Goal - 42-yarder by Matt Stover. 10:13 remaining. (4 plays, 7 yards. Time of Drive: 1:13). Baltimore Safety - Michael McCrary tackles Curtis Martin in end

zone. 6:21 remaining. - Baltimore Touchdown - 98-yard interception return by Chris McAlister. (Jamal Lewis run). 0:08 remaining.

3rd Quarter — New York Field Goal - 40-yarder by Brett Conway. 10:58 remaining. (7 plays, 42 yards. Time of Drive: 2:03
Baltimore Touchdown - 54-yard punt return by Jermaine Lewis. (Matt Stover kick). 6:19 remaining.

4th Quarter — New York Field Goal - 19-yarder by Brett Conway. 13:38 remaining. (10 plays, 35 yards. Time of Drive: 3:08). - Baltimore Touchdown - 90-yard punt return by Jermaine Lewis. (Matt Stover kick). 5:02 remaining.

FINAL TEAM STATISTICS

	New York	Baltimore
First Downs	22	5
Rushes-Yards	21-51	26-64
Passing Yards	473	78
Return Yards	46	374
Punts-Average	6-49.7	10-42.2
Fumbles-Lost	4-3	3-0
Penalties-Yards	4-19	5-32
Time of Possession	32:14	27:46

Ravens vs. Broncos

SCORE BY QUARTERS

TEAM	1	2	3	4	OT	SCORE
Denver	0	3	0	0		3
Baltimore	0	14	7	0		21

SCORING SUMMARY

1st Quarter — No scoring.

2nd Quarter — Baltimore Touchdown - 1-yard run by Jamal Lewis. (Matt Stover kick). 11:43 remaining. (10 plays, 75 yards. Time of Drive: 5:51).
Denver Field Goal - 31-yarder by Jason Elam. 4:31 remaining. (12 plays, 68 yards. Time of Drive: 7:12).
Baltimore Touchdown - 58-yard pass from Trent Dilfer to Shannon Sharpe. (Matt Stover kick). 4:06 remaining. (1 play, 58 yards. Time of Drive: 0:25).

3rd Quarter — Baltimore Touchdown - 27-yard run by Jamal Lewis. (Matt Stover kick). 3:19 remaining. (2 plays, 28 yards. Time of Drive: 0:42).

4th Quarter — No scoring.

FINAL TEAM STATISTICS

	Denver	Baltimore
First Downs	9	13
Rushes-Yards	18-42	38-122
Passing Yards	135	118
Return Yards	13	30
Passing (Att-Comp-Int)	38-18-1	15-9-0
Punts-Average	9-38.4	10-38.3
Fumbles-Lost	0-0	1-0
Penalties-Yards	6-33	4-30
Time of Possession	27:37	32:23

Ravens vs. Titans

SCORE BY QUARTERS

TEAM	1	2	3	4	OT	SCORE
Baltimore	0	7	3	14		24
Tennessee	7	0	3	0		10

SCORING SUMMARY

1st Quarter — Tennessee Touchdown - 2-yard run by Eddie George. (Al Del Greco kick). 7:43 remaining. (11 plays, 68 yards. Time of Drive: 7:17).

2nd Quarter — Baltimore Touchdown - 1-yard run by Jamal Lewis. (Matt Stover kick). 9:46 remaining. (4 plays, 57 yards. Time of Drive: 1:36).

3rd Quarter — Tennessee Field Goal - 21-yarder by Al Del Greco. 8:20 remaining. (8 plays, 24 yards. Time of Drive: 4:17). - Baltimore Field Goal - 38-yarder by Matt Stover. 3:05 remaining. (6 plays, 25 yards. Time of Drive: 2:34).

4th Quarter — Baltimore Touchdown - 90-yard blocked field goal return by Anthony Mitchell. (Matt Stover kick). 12:12 remaining. - Baltimore Touchdown - 50-yard interception return by Ray Lewis. (Matt Stover kick). 6:41 remaining.

FINAL TEAM STATISTICS

	Baltimore	Tennessee
First Downs	6	23
Rushes-Yards	23-49	33-126
Passing Yards	85	191
Return Yards	54	5
Passing (Att-Comp-Int)	17-5-0	47-25-1
Punts-Average	8-27.6	5-37.8
Fumbles-Lost	0-0	0-0
Penalties-Yards	7-50	6-55
Time of Possession	19:31	40:29

Ravens vs. Raiders

SCORE BY QUARTERS

TEAM	1	2	3	4	OT	SCORE
Baltimore	0	10	3	3		16
Oakland	0	0	3	0		3

SCORING SUMMARY

1st Quarter — No scoring.

2nd Quarter — Baltimore Touchdown - 96-yard pass from Trent Dilfer to Shannon Sharpe. (Matt Stover kick). 11:08 remaining. (3 plays, 88 yards. Time of Drive: 1:27).
Baltimore Field Goal - 31-yarder by Matt Stover. 8:19 remaining. (4 plays, 8 yards. Time of Drive: 1:53).

3rd Quarter — Oakland Field Goal - 24-yarder by Sebastian Janikowski. 10:07 remaining. (9 plays 34 yards. Time of Drive: 3:37).
Baltimore Field Goal - 29-yarder by Matt Stover. 5:08 remaining. (9 plays, 61 yards. Time of Drive: 4:48).

4th Quarter — Baltimore Field Goal - 21-yarder by Matt Stover. 7:28 remaining. (7 plays, 4 yards. Time of Drive: 4:03).

FINAL TEAM STATISTICS

	Baltimore	Oakland
First Downs	12	12
Rushes-Yards	46-110	17-24
Passing Yards	172	167
Return Yards	117	11
Passing (Att-Comp-Int)	18-9-1	37-19-4
Punts-Average	7-40.6	7-45.0
Fumbles-Lost	2-1	2-1
Penalties-Yards	10-95	5-36
Time of Possession	34:38	25:22

Ravens vs. Giants

TEAM	1	2	3	4	OT	SCORE
Baltimore	7	3	14	10		34
NY Giants	0	0	7	0		7

SCORING SUMMARY

1st Quarter — Baltimore Touchdown - 38-yard pass from Trent Dilfer to Brandon Stokley. (Matt Stover kick). 6:50 remaining. (2 plays, 41 yards. Time of Drive: 0:45).

2nd Quarter — Baltimore Field Goal - 47-yarder by Matt Stover. 1:41 remaining. (7 plays, 59 yards. Time of Drive: 2:28).

3rd Quarter — Baltimore Touchdown - 49-yard interception return by Duane Starks. (Matt Stover kick). 3:49 remaining.
New York Touchdown - 97-yard kickoff return by Ron Dixon. (Brad Daluiso kick). 3:31 remaining.
Baltimore Touchdown - 84-yard kickoff return by Jermaine Lewis. (Matt Stover kick). 3:13 remaining.

4th Quarter — Baltimore Touchdown - 3-yard run by Jamal Lewis. (Matt Stover kick). 8:45 remaining. (6 plays, 38 yards. Time of Drive: 4:17).
Baltimore Field Goal - 34-yarder by Matt Stover. 5:27 remaining. (5 plays, 18 yards. Time of Drive: 3:02).

FINAL TEAM STATISTICS

	Baltimore	New York
First Downs	13	11
Rushes-Yards	33-111	16-66
Passing Yards	133	86
Return Yards	93	46
Passing (Att-Comp-Int)	26-12-0	39-15-4
Punts-Average	10-43.0	11-38.4
Fumbles-Lost	2-0	2-1
Penalties-Yards	9-70	6-27
Time of Possession	34:06	25:54